JACK HINTON V.C.

J D Hinton VC

Also by Gabrielle McDonald

New Zealand's Secret Heroes

JACK HINTON V.C.
A MAN AMONGST MEN

Gabrielle McDonald

David Ling Publishing Limited
PO Box 34-601
Birkenhead, Auckland 10

Jack Hinton V.C.
First Edition

ISBN 0-908990-43-X

First Published 1997

Typeset by ExPress Communications Limited
Printed in New Zealand

– CONTENTS –

DEDICATION

This book is dedicated to the memory of my beloved Mother and Father who sadly did not live to see this manuscript in print.

Rosemary Bernadette Jones 9/2/26 – 24/6/96
Kenneth Richard Jones 12/9/21 – 14/1/96

And also to the memory of my dear friend, the late Basil Borthwick, formerly of 20 Battalion, who taught me so much, and without whose help this book could not have been written.

"For some we loved, the loveliest and the best
That from this Vintage rolling Time has prest,
Have drunk their cup a Round or two before,
And one by one crept silently to rest."
– Omar Khayyam –

FOREWORD

The volunteers who made up the early echelons of the 2nd Expeditionary Force were remarkable men. Life in New Zealand between the two World Wars, particularly during the Great Depression, had for many been hard. Working conditions, particularly on farms or in the bush, were harsh. Welfare was scanty. People had to fend for themselves. Those who came through those years tend to emerge as men as resource, self-reliant, tough, and responsible. These were the qualities which were to fit them admirably for the war which broke out in 1939. Jack Hinton was one of these men. Born in Colac Bay, near Riverton, in 1909, the son of a railwayman, he grew up in Southland at a time when conditions there were stern, when much of the rich farmland of today was sour soil in the need of drainage and fertilisers.

Jack Hinton quickly showed his readiness to face the challenge of these conditions. When only a youth he went to sea as a cabin boy on a Norwegian whaling ship, one of the many operating out of the Stewart Island. He spent nine months on an expedition to the Antarctic, which took the ship through seas abounding in icebergs, in pursuit of whales. It was a life of danger and hardship – and of the stench of whale blubber, a smell which still lingered on these whaling vessels when they returned to Paterson Inlet.

Other jobs, typical of the pattern of work in those days, followed – mustering on sheep stations; black sanding for gold; working as a stable lad in a horse racing stable; road building. On a West Coast road gang Jack Hinton rose to the rank of foreman – invaluable training in leading men.

When war broke out in 1939 Jack Hinton volunteered immediately, even though he was too old for front line soldiering. He was soon a sergeant in what was to become the famous 20 Battalion, commanded by Colonel Howard Kippenberger, who was to become a legendary figure in the 2nd NZ Division.

By April 1941 the Division was in Greece. Sergeant Hinton was put in charge of a draft of reinforcements for the 20th, camping under the pine trees south of Athens, held in readiness to fill the gaps which, it was expected, would soon be torn in the ranks of the Battalion. But the British and Commonwealth forces, facing overwhelming German opposition, particularly in the air, were soon in retreat.

The main body of the Division was successfully evacuated from ports on the east coast of Attica. But the reinforcements were directed, for evacuation, to the port of Kalamata, in the Peloponnese. Before the Royal Navy could take them off, the Germans reached the port. It was in fighting to hold a bridgehead, so that the evacuation could take place, that Jack Hinton showed the valour which won him the Victoria Cross. It was a particularly high form of valour, because this was the first time he had been in action, and he went into the battle, not as part of an organised fighting unit, but as part of a scratch force made up of men from several different forces, under commanders who saw the task as hopeless, and saw no option but to surrender. But surrender was not something that occurred to Jack Hinton. He quickly joined those who decided to counterattack, and led the onslaught with vigour and skill until he was wounded and taken prisoner.

I read Gabrielle McDonald's vivid account of the battle with particular interest, as, but for a quirk of fate, I would have been caught up in it myself. I had been in the same Reinforcements Camp outside Athens as Jack Hinton. We slept under the umbrella pines, and mounted patrols at night to guard Athens airport from parachutist attacks. But I had gone forward to the Division five days before, and with the front collapsing, the reinforcements were ordered to Kalamata. I was evacuated with the main body, and was in Crete when I heard of the disaster of Kalamata, and realised by what a slim margin I too had been spared the fate of finding myself a POW for the rest of the war.

Gabrielle McDonald has told, with admirable clarity and insight, the tale not only of Jack Hinton, the man, but of the times in which he lived, of the New Zealand of the 1920s and 1930s which had shaped him, which produced this soldier who, given only one chance to fight, did so with consummate daring. This is a story not just of a remarkable individual, but of the New Zealand of his day. Rightly she has called it a tale of "A Man Amongst Men". And what men they were, those Kiwis of the division from whose ranks emerged figures like Jack Hinton and Charles Upham, the double V.C., Lieutenant Ngarimu V.C., Major-General Sir Howard Kippenberger, DSO and Bar, and a host of others who truly matched themselves to the hour. This book, by recording Jack Hinton's contribution to that hall of fame, is not only highly readable, but is a valuable addition to the story of New Zealand.

Sir Geoffrey Cox

INTRODUCTION AND ACKNOWLEDGEMENTS

Some readers will wonder why I, a woman, and one who was born after World War II finished, should write on such a subject. It began a long time ago when I was perhaps 8 or 9 years of age. I had heard a lot about the war. Both my grandfathers had fought in it, as well as my father, and my maternal grandfather had lost his life in the Western Desert. His death affected my family in a profound way. My grandmother, mother and uncle had lost a loved husband and father, and I lived with a feeling of sadness throughout my childhood.

When I was about 10 I began to read as much as I could about the war. While my friends were reading Girls Own I was avidly devouring books on war heroes, battles and secret agents. I also saw every war movie I could. This fascination with World War II carried on throughout my teen years, eventually culminating in a career as a journalist and war historian.

I first met Jack Hinton in 1989 when I wrote an article on him for the Christchurch Star. He had fought with 20 Battalion, in the same battalion as my grandfather had fought in. I realised he had lived a fascinating life, and I was very proud when I was asked to write his life story.

In the three years or so it has taken to write this book, I have met many interesting people, and it is to them that I owe my gratitude. I want to thank particularly Jack and Molly who gave me so much of their time. Often we sat until the small hours while Molly made never-ending cups of coffee to keep us awake.

I am indebted to the men of the 20 Battalion and Armoured Regiment; the late Basil Borthwick who never failed to encourage me in this project, the late Brigadier Jim Burrows, Bill (Fox), Allison, the late Allen Forrester, Trevor Blaker, the late Noel

Cameron, Frank Helm, Mervyn Wallace, the late Charles Upham V.C. and Bar, Jim McDevitt, Jim Moodie, Doug Eggelton, and Eric Townley in Melbourne, who supplied me with the humorous incidents.

Thanks also to Peter Scott for his ongoing encouragement, and to John Mitchell in Auckland, to Major General Piers Read of the New Zealand Army for supplying documents, to Len Pitcher, Don Miles, the late Lindsay Abbie, Tom Findlay, the late Joe Simpson, Albie Thompson, Tom Scanlan, Fritz Hahn in Germany, Bill Diedrichs, Derek Jones and Jim Patterson. In Australia to Bruce Hewitt and Sid Bishop, and Edward Heath and Bob Prouse in Canada. A thank you to John Parera in Chrisstchurch for supplying valuable photographs.

I am also indebted to Sir Geoffrey Cox in England for his advice on my manuscript and for writing the Foreword, to Edward Howell for permission to quote from Escape to Live, to Blue Glue in Nelson for his encouragement, his advice, his reading, correcting and editing much of the work, and finally for permission to quote from his writings, and from 20 Battalion and Armoured Regiment.

I wish to add that I have leaned heavily on the war histories for assistance in writing the chapters on Greece.

Finally I received invaluable assistance from Geoff Rothwell in the Bay of Islands who typed the whole manuscript, putting it on disk, and for his continual encouragement and support. To my publisher David Ling, my good friends, Adi, Annette and Dulcie, and to all my family, both in New Zealand and Australia – thank you for your continued love and support.

This book could not have been written without the help from all these people, and what I owe them is beyond evaluation.

THE VICTORIA CROSS

The Victoria Cross is the highest award for bravery. It has been awarded to only 1350 men, three of whom have won it twice – Captain Charles Upham of New Zealand in World War II, and two doctors, Lt. A. Martin-Leake in the South African war and Captain N.G. Chavasse in World War I.

The deeds for which the V.C. has been won are as varied as the backgrounds from which the winners have come. For it is the most democratic of all medals, open not only to the private soldier but also to his commanding officer. In Queen Victoria's own words:

> "...it should be highly prized and eagerly sought after above all others, and awarded regardless of rank, long service, wounds or any other circumstance or condition save the merit of bravery which alone should establish sufficient claim to the honour."

The V.C. is a bronze cross 1 1/2 inches across with a purple ribbon and an inscription which says simply "FOR VALOUR". The bronze on the cross is cast from the cannons captured at Sevastopol in the Crimean War. It retains a mystique that no other decoration has ever achieved. It has never been won by a woman, although the rules do not preclude that possibility, yet it has been awarded to four civilians, contrary to popular belief. Two Germans have won it, as well as one Russian and five Americans. It has been conferred upon every rank of soldier, although Captain Upham has been the only combatant to win it twice.

It has been won in every war and campaign in which British and Commonwealth forces have fought, from the Crimean War in 1854 to the Falklands War.

The main requirement for winning the V.C. remains conspicuous bravery. It cannot be earned in any other way, whether by influence or privilege.

The Duke of Windsor, when he was Prince of Wales, proclaimed it to be "the most democratic, and at the same time the most exclusive of all orders of chivalry – the Most Enviable Order of the Victoria Cross."

Jack Hinton was the first New Zealander in World War II to win this most coveted of all medals. He came from Southland and showed distinctive qualities of resource and initiative. He had typical Kiwi strength of purpose and determination. He was of a tough and unyielding personality, and refused to accept defeat. As a result he was prepared to fight until he dropped.

This is not only the story of how Jack Hinton won the V.C. It is the story of an extraordinary man who has lived an extraordinary life – one of hardship and adventure.

Jack Hinton is our last surviving Victoria Cross winner.

Seven other New Zealanders won the V.C. during World War II:

Charles Upham, V.C. and Bar
Alfred Clive Hulme
James Allen Ward
Keith Elliott
Moana Nui-a-Kiwa Ngarimu
Leonard Henry Trent, D.F.C.
Lloyd Allan Trigg, D.F.C.

PROLOGUE

28 APRIL, 1941 KALAMATA, NORTHERN GREECE

The streets were darkening in the small seaside town of Kalamata in Greece. It was 1941 and the war in Europe was some 19 months' old. The New Zealanders had been in Greece for six weeks as reinforcements to help the Greek nation rout the Germans as quickly as possible from their beloved country. Greek resistance had crumbled swiftly as the Germans occupied all of Greece, and retreat and evacuation of allied troops had to be done as quickly as possible. The Germans had captured all the evacuation beaches and ports except Kalamata. It was at Kalamata that the New Zealand troops were waiting – part of a force of 8,000 men awaiting the evacuation ships.

A tall, thin New Zealander emerged suddenly from the cover of darkness of a doorway of a white-washed house by the quay. A .303 rifle with fixed bayonet was in his hand, while several hand grenades were in his trouser pocket, ready to be used at a moment's notice. His face was tense and streaked with dirt. It was grey with tiredness as he had not slept for several days, but it was grimly set and determined. One could imagine by the look of him that he would not let anyone, or anything, get in his way.

Jack Hinton, a 31-year-old from Colac Bay, Southland, looked up and down the street. He could hear the sound of firing from the big guns on the Kalamata waterfront. The air was thick with dust and fumes. Mortar bombs were exploding everywhere. The street was now darkening rapidly except for streams of tracer bullets, and the sudden clarity after a flare goes up.

The New Zealander knew he must act quickly, but he must be careful. He must not panic. He knew there were pockets of stray Germans hidden in the doorways of the houses all around him. Almost in answer to these thoughts, out of the corner of his eye he suddenly spotted the grey-blue of a German uniform. Without warning the German opened fire, wounding several New Zealanders with a burst from his machine gun. Confusion reigned everywhere – there was no overall command.

"Dammit!" the man muttered to himself. He just had to get to the waterfront and knock those guns out before they did any more damage, and before any more of his mates were wounded.

"Give me covering fire!" he shouted to Private Alan Jones from Invercargill. Jones immediately ran down the street with him, covering Hinton with fire from his Bren gun. With one swift movement Hinton smashed open the door of a house with his boot, threw a handful of grenades inside, and then continued down the street with Jones behind him.

As fast as possible the two men turned on to the waterfront, a blur in front of them now, with machine-gun fire and dust from the heavy mortars exploding all around them. Sweat from the warm Greek night trickled down Hinton's back, leaving a dark stain on his khaki shirt. The sweat stung his eyes. He didn't wipe it away – there was no time for that. He had to keep going.

Meanwhile a truck loaded with Australian and New Zealand troops turned on to the waterfront and pulled up sharply with a squeal of tyres. Men jumped from the truck and dashed to cover the nearest side street, opening fire on the Germans who were grouped about the guns and along the quay.

Everywhere was chaos. Shouted commands could be heard and men could be seen running back to the safety of the olive groves.

Major Basil Carey from the 3rd Tank Regiment was lying in a slit trench together with Major Pemberton of the Royal Signals. At intervals Carey would fire at the German guns on the quay.

"Come on!" he'd shout to some of the Allied soldiers. "Who wants to fight with me?"

He saw Hinton, who had just reached a group of Allied soldiers. "I'll give you covering fire if you'll put out those bloody guns!" said Carey.

Hinton knew that the Major was right. Something had to be done and quickly. Anger boiled inside him. He didn't hesitate. He ran to within several metres of the nearest gun. His heart thumped painfully in his chest, but he kept on running, throwing the last of his grenades as he went. As if in a dream he could hear the cries of the wounded, smell the gunpowder. He knew Private Jones and the others were with him – he could hear their shouts.

"If I can just wipe that lot out over there" he told himself "then I can sleep." Sleep, precious sleep. But he musn't think about it. Keep going, keep going. He didn't see the German run out of the building. He didn't even see him lift his Spandau and fire point-blank at him. He saw just a quick flash of field-grey as he felt something hit his stomach. He looked down and saw blood spurting from his abdomen. In the same moment he felt waves of nausea sweep over him. There was no pain, just a warm feeling, as his legs buckled under him and the sky grew darker in front of his eyes.

–1–
THE EARLY YEARS

**"I CONSIDER IT THE BEST PART OF AN
EDUCATION TO HAVE BEEN BORN AND BROUGHT
UP IN THE COUNTRY."**

– ALCOTT –

John Daniel Hinton was born on 17 September 1909 at Colac
Bay, Southland. Colac Bay is a small seaside resort, and even
today it has hardly changed. At the turn of the century it had two
sawmills, some flax mills, three farms, approximately 30 houses,
one hotel, a church, and a school attended by both Maori and
Pakeha. The name is an English corruption of the Maori Ko-
oraka, probably from the time when Maori pronunciation in
Southland had certain peculiarities not found elsewhere in New
Zealand. Ko-oraka means "place of Raka", Raka being a local
chieftain. Today, Colac Bay is listed as a small bay on the northern
shoreline of Foveaux Strait, 12 kms west of Riverton, 50 kms
west of Invercargill, Southland. It is a small farming community,
with a Post Office, licensed hotel, restaurant-tearooms, and a
motor camp with cabin accommodation close to the beach.

Jack was the fifth child of Harry Godfrey Hinton and his wife
Mary Elizabeth. Both his parents, of Scottish and Irish descent,
had been born close to Colac Bay – his father, Harry, who had
served in the Boer War, at Invercargill, and his mother, Mary, just
outside of the Bay itself. Jack had five sisters – Nellie, Christine,
Frances, Effie, and Elmore, and one brother, Charles. He has
outlived them all.

Nellie married Milan Pupich. They lived on the West Coast
and had a farm near Lyell.

Christine was known as Chris. She married a farmer, Jack
Ford, and they lived in Fairfax, Southland.

Charles, the only other son, was a coalminer on the West Coast.

Frances was known as Fanny. She married Ernest John Leckie, an ironmonger. She lived in Southland all her life.

Effie married Walter O'Toole and lived in Southland all her life.

Elmore was the youngest of the family. She was married first to William Holmes and lived in Christchurch, and later married a physiotherapist.

Life was very hard in those days and money was short. New Zealand was still a new country and life was very much as it was in the pioneering days. However, people were optimistic, and as journalist T.P. McLean has written since: "...Marching into the twentieth century, New Zealand, and New Zealanders, could be said to be engrossed, above all else, in politics, war and sport."

In 1901 a national census had proclaimed that there were 815,583 men, women and children permanent residents in New Zealand. In the early days of the 20th century large families of six or more children were not uncommon. On the farm a man would often work 10 to 12 hours a day, sowing pastures, tending flocks or herds and burning and clearing land. Often the milk had to be separated by hand into cream and whey. It was hardship to a great degree. There was no transport other than horse and cart until the 1920s, which brought far-reaching changes in New Zealand life. There was also no electricity until 1929. With the advent of power, domestic life was totally transformed.

In the warm summer months during his early childhood, Jack and his brother Charles would supplement the family income by selling sea eggs to tourists. Together with the other Pakeha children, they would sell supplejacks, which resembled vines from bushes, and the tourists would use these for walking sticks on bush walks.

Once a fortnight the silent movies would come to Colac Bay. This would cause great excitement, especially amongst the children. The movies would be shown in the little town hall, and anyone who wanted to carry the water to make the machine engines turn would get a free ticket. Jack was always keen to do this. He would go over the railway lines to fetch the water in an old kerosene tin borrowed from his father's garden shed.

As well as the old silent movies, exciting travelling acts would arrive in the Bay – magicians, vaudeville artists, fortune tellers, and various concert players. They would entertain the local folk for a minimal price – Henry French, the magician, charged only tuppence to see his show.

In 1914 at the age of five, Jack started at the small Colac Bay School. The school, attended by both Maori and Pakeha, went up to Standard 6, and those children who wanted to achieve higher education went on to the High School at Invercargill.

One of the teachers who taught at the local primary school was a very beautiful young girl, known to the children as Miss Frederick. She also taught music privately, and Jack, who was a little in love with her, wished with all his heart that he could be taught music by her as well. She would ride a bike around the Bay with a small piano balanced on the handle bars. The mischievous Jack, always looking for ways to make a quick bob, and also to see her, of course, and keep in her good books, would steal her bicycle pump, and then pretend to find it again. The grateful school teacher would reward him with a shilling or two.

Riverton is about 12km from Colac Bay, and in the main street was Nell Hunt's shop which sold everything from a needle to an anchor. Nell would also sell house-to-house in the Bay. The young Jack and his mates were always on the scrounge to find suitable items to give to Nell to sell on their behalf. Money, however, was always a problem, and sometimes Jack would steal vegetables from his father's garden to sell.

Harry Hinton was a strict disciplinarian. He worked for the New Zealand Railways, and was to stay with them for over 33 years. Most of his spare time was spent in his garden and his large family always had fresh vegetables and fruit on their table.

Jack adored his mother, who was always loving and kind-hearted towards her children, and he would do anything for her. Knowing money was short, he applied for a job at Harrison's, a local farm. Every morning before he went to school he would milk the cows. There were about 40 cows and he would separate the milk by hand, wash their udders by hand, run off to school, and then return to the job after school finished for the day. All his pay would go to his mother – about 2/6d a month.

But it wasn't all work and no play. On weekends, the Hintons would often go floundering, taking an old pram for the fish. They would use a large seine net to catch the flounder. Jack and Charles, in particular, would love these weekends.

On some Saturdays the family would go to Wakamatu Beach where they would catch freshwater crayfish, or crawlies, as they were called. These crawlies were tasty to eat, and they were always shared with the rest of the fishing families in the district. Very often mussels, pauas and cockles from off the rocks were added to the catch. There would be four men to a net, and local Maori from the kike, or village, would often join the Hintons.

Jack was fascinated watching the Maori catch muttonbirds. They would go around the Hinenui Point at Colac Bay to catch the birds. When the birds were caught they would be packed in kits made from big bull kelp, which would be protected with totara bark. These kits, which contained anything from 25 – 300 muttonbirds, would be sold in various towns. They were oily, but quite tasty to eat.

"The muttonbirds feed on sardines" said Jack. "I reckon some of the best sardines in the world were caught in those early days."

The kelp kits went into flax baskets which had been made by the Maori, and these baskets protected the kelp. Jack still remembers what an amazing sight it was watching the muttonbirds coming up from the islands by the hundreds and thousands. The birds chased the sardines, filled their crops, and then flew home to their burrows and to their young. When the birds were chasing the sardines the last wave would leave them stranded on the beach, and that would be the ideal time to catch them.

"We would often make cricket balls out of the kelp," says Jack. "And we would watch the Maori boiling the muttonbirds with vinegar, pepper and butter."

The local kids also fished for butterfish off the rocks. Jack can still taste and smell those delicious fish today.

As well as fishing for crawlies and eels, the Colac Bay children occasionally went to Ruapuke Island, which was close to Colac Bay. They went there and to Stewart Island and Centre Island for picnics and to look at the wild horses. The horses were eventually sold to circuses.

About a kilometre from Colac Bay was Round Hill – a great little mining town. It had a hydraulic blow-up system for gold, which was one of the biggest in the Southern Hemisphere. Round Hill, as well as Colac Bay, was full of Chinese who worked there. They had strange names like One-eyed Sam, Hop-a-long, Peg-legged Sam, and Jimmy-the-one. Round Hill had one hotel, a Chinese joss-house, and a communal church used by all denominations. It was at Round Hill that Jack first met Bill Thomas, and saw him again years later when he was a farmer in Methven.

When the weather became cooler the adults would go to Lake George, halfway between Colac Bay and Round Hill, to shoot wild ducks and swans. The lake was a great fishing spot for crawlies and eels, and the children often fished there while their parents went shooting.

As Jack grew older, he was given more responsibility at Harrison's farm. One of his new jobs was to wash all the eggs for market. One day, Mrs Harrison's daughter, Hui, who was a great singer and pianist, and who also played for the mobile picture man, put her head out of the bedroom window and started to sing. This infuriated Jack for some reason, and he yelled at her to "Shut up!" Hui carried on, taking no notice at all, so he picked up a piece of soap and threw it at her. It hit her in the eye, and Jack took off for home very quickly that day! Of course, he wasn't very keen to return to the farm for some time after that.

Years later, Jack, together with his friend Del Fea from Invercargill and his wife Molly, spent his 79th birthday with Hui, who was then living in Invercargill. Did she remember the soap incident? Indeed she did, but there were no hard feelings, and they spent Jack's birthday with great hilarity recalling those years of long ago.

Jack was always full of mischief, and sometimes took detonators from where his father worked at the railways, and put them on the railway lines to see what would happen. His schoolmates, of course, would join in the fun, and there was 'hell to pay' when they were caught.

Living in a small place like Colac Bay, close to nature, Jack very quickly learned about animals, birds and insects. There were many wild bees in those days. They lived mostly in rata trees and manuka flowers, and Jack and his friends smoked them out with green manuka. Then they would take the honeycomb back home to make honey.

They also set traps for rabbits with great success, which meant the families quite often ate rabbit twice a day. It was a good source of food. There were also wild pigeons and possums in the Bay, so there was always plenty to eat.

The First World War between 1914-1918 didn't seem to affect the Hinton family greatly. Harry Hinton did not go away to war so their lives basically carried on the same. However, other families in the district were affected personally as was most of the country. As well as the physical hardships of the early years at the turn of the century, New Zealanders had to cope not only with the huge losses from the war, but with the devastating influenza epidemic of 1918 which added further to the losses. These losses cast shadows of gloom over the whole country which lasted well into the mid-1920s. From a total which represented some 45 per cent of New Zealand men of military age, 16,700 died in service. Casualties exceeded 58,000. On top of all that the death toll from the flu epidemic was 5,516. However, New Zealanders are renowned for their toughness and their ability to bounce back. They kept their spirits up by partaking in sport, singing and dancing. Music is a great panacea for melancholia and the New Zealanders could lose themselves in some of the lovely old romantic ballads of the early 1920s. At every opportunity they would frequent the dance halls and dance to the strains of "Swanee", "Among My Souvenirs", "Somebody Loves Me", and a little later the popular ballad "Ramona".

In 1921, at the age of 12, Jack left the Colac Bay school. In the words of his teacher, Mr Brown, who taught the standards: "There's nothing more I can teach you, Hinton!"

Around the same time – Jack can't remember exactly – he ran

23

away from home. This would be a major event in any boy's life, certainly one as young as Jack. It left an indelible impression on his mind. It was also to shape and mould his character. Some twenty years later people all over the world would hear the name Jack Hinton. The name would be synonymous with the words "resourceful, tough, single-minded, and determined."

–2–
GROWING UP IN THE DEPRESSION

"THE COUNTRY FOR A WOUNDED HEART"
– AN OLD ENGLISH PROVERB –

It was 1921. There was much unemployment, surging land prices, and a high cost of living in New Zealand. People were still recovering from the huge loss of life during World War I and the influenza epidemic. All these factors influenced New Zealand society. However, people had a healthy respect for hard work, law and order and decency. There was an ideal which persisted in New Zealand that this was a country "fit for heroes to live in."

After the war had finished in 1918 the Government had spent about 26 million pounds in settling returned soldiers on farms. Some prospered, others just broke even, while some were obliged to give up. After being told by his teacher that there was nothing further that he could teach him, and after an argument with his father, Jack decided to run away from home. He knew he had to earn money to live, and the first thing he did was to look for a job. He managed to find one with the grocer in Tokanui, about 50 kilometres from Invercargill. The job entailed driving a three-horse wagon, which sold everything – fencing wire, nails, groceries of all types. He was paid 5/- a week, and he delivered to all the farm houses. He also collected eggs from the farms and separated butter.

Although the horse and buggy era was at an end, wagons and carts were still commonplace in rural areas, and in the small town of Tokanui it was rare to see one of the new motor vehicles. If one did happen to pass through, the locals would rush out and stare fascinated as it went on its way.

Jack did not stay long in Tokanui and in 1922 sailed to the Ross Sea on a Norwegian whaling ship, the *C.A. Larsen*. The *Larsen* was a factory ship with a displacement of 15,000 tonnes. It was, at one time, the largest whale factory ship in the world. It was 158 metres long, 9.9 metres deep, with a 20 metre beam. The deck fittings complied with all the requirements of whaling, and below deck was a profusion of machinery – pipes, tanks, machines and even large grindstones to keep the blubber flensing knives sharp.

All the Norwegian whalers were termed "floating factories". In the 1920s several whaling ships under the command of the Norwegian Captain Carl Anton Larsen, and belonging to the Rosshavet Whaling Company, steamed regularly into Paterson Inlet, the beautiful protected harbour of Stewart Island. This was a popular haven for the whaling ships and an obvious choice for Antarctic whalers who needed to make winter repairs to their ships. The whalers, who had lived a hard, tough life on the ships, were overjoyed to spend some time in the lush green paradise of Stewart Island while repairs were made. Many of the Norwegians later settled in Stewart Island and raised families. Today, their children and grandchildren are still there.

Jack had heard many stories about whaling. He knew that whales had been hunted for centuries, and that the whaling season lasted between seven and nine months. Ships left their bases usually at the beginning of October and returned in April or May. Hunting usually lasted from January until about the end of March. The largest whale is four times the length of a bus, and a fully grown blue whale measures over 30 metres in length.

Antarctic whales were worth a great deal of money and Jack had heard that the whalers were well paid. Antarctic whaling expeditions hunted the blue whale, the rorqual or finback whale and the cachalot.

Jack also had a strong sense of adventure, and the thought of going to the Ross Sea filled him with excitement. He was thrilled when he was hired as a galleyhand. He was the youngest boy on the boat, and he wondered, when he signed on, whether he should let his parents know what he was going to do. He finally decided not to tell them because he felt sure they would stop him from going.

The grey-blue *Larsen* left at dawn the day after Jack had signed on. As it steamed out of Paterson Inlet, Jack could not help but wonder if he had done the right thing.

He watched as preparations took place for the great task ahead. The men were nailing wooden planks onto the floors of the gangways as well as the decks. This was to protect the decks from blubber and blood trodden in by the men's heavy boots.

Jack worked twelve hours a day seven days a week, mainly washing pots and pans and doing odd jobs on the ship. In return he had free meals and clothing, including some heavy winter underclothes. The whalers all wore peaked caps and thick work clothes which they wore continuously. If Jack had thought he had a tough life before, he was in for a shock on the *Larsen*. The Ross Sea was treacherous and unpredictable and they were constantly fighting the elements. There were always gales and blizzards, and a few weeks into their journey Jack awoke to raging seas battering against the hull. As the men came on deck for a moment they clung to the ship's rails, their breath coming in great gasps as a vicious wind whipped around them fiercely. They pointed out to one another the foam-spattered whale catchers which danced madly over the rolling green waters.

Down below in the galley Jack clung to one of the rails in the kitchen, his stomach heaving. The storm eventually died down, and the sea gradually changed to a greyer colour. When he thought everything had returned to normal, he had his first unexpected sighting of an iceberg. It loomed in front of him, filling him with fear for the first time in his life. It appeared in the form of a glittering mountain – jagged, irregular in shape and beaten by the waves. Jack had never seen anything so huge. He was rigid with fear, and he could not take his eyes off the enormous white shape with its tinge of blue. It seemed to Jack that the ship passed perilously close, even though it was several hundred metres away. Despite the distance, the air grew suddenly colder as the ship passed by.

The *Larsen* then cruised into colder waters, and the nights became shorter. One day Jack, going up on deck during a break from his work, noticed he could not distinguish between sky or sea. A milky whiteness enclosed the ship on all sides. Even the whale catchers had disappeared into the mist. It took three days before the mist cleared. The rigging was covered with a thick white frost which sparkled like diamonds in the early morning sun.

Jack looked out over the vast expanse of waters. There was nothing to be seen except the large blue and white icebergs. There was no wildlife of any description and the air was perfectly still. He stood quietly gazing out at the scene in front of him. The fear he had felt earlier had now been replaced by something else – it was a feeling of wonder and awe at the beauty around him. For several more days the *Larsen* steamed on. The days were long with shorter and shorter intervals between them. Twilight lasted longer and longer, and at last Jack saw an unbroken line on the horizon. The *Larsen* could move no further south – it had struck icy water.

A lookout man shouted – a shout to wake any harpooner. A blue whale had been sighted. It is, however, a champion swimmer. When in flight, it can do 20 knots. The whale catcher can do 18, if the sea is not running against it. Orders were shouted loudly in Norwegian. Bells rang and winches began to turn. Just as Jack saw the huge tail of a whale rise out of the water, followed by the rest of its body, a fierce wind blew up.

Some of the other men seemed just as excited as Jack. They had seen hundreds of whales hunted before, but it never ceased to fill them with excitement. The whale had a muscular strength so formidable that it could make its way easily through storms. Now Jack watched it fight for its life. One of the men fired the gun, aiming it just behind the whale's head. The whale was barely 50 metres away from the boat, and now it swam to more than 300 metres from the bows of the boat. It tried to tow the chaser which followed it, slowing down its progress. Jack instinctively knew that the blue whale, once it had been harpooned, had very little chance of escaping, as the harpoon, fired into it like a shell, buries itself completely in the animal's flesh. The harpoon used to kill the whale consisted of a tube open at both ends. It ejected a rocket, which carried the harpoon and its line.

The men began to get the cables and chains ready. Jack watched from afar, fascinated. He wanted to do something to help but knew it would not be allowed. The men were now working at a frantic pace, realising that with such a tempestuous sea they could lose the whale at any moment. The line sagged a little and then rose slowly. It would be impossible to heave to. Everything would have to be done at the windlass. The men would have to pull in the line, let it go again, and pull it in once more. Watching the men do this, Jack was reminded of the times when he had seen his father fishing for salmon, manipulating his rod.

The whale suddenly reappeared, moving very slowly. One of the men shouted excitedly: "Got you, my girl! Got you!"

It certainly looked as if he was right. To Jack, the whale looked completely exhausted. Less than a minute after surfacing, it was motionless on the water, breathing blood. Jack stared at the dying animal as he watched its breath turn pink, then red, the wind blowing a great shower of blood in the faces of the men. To the young 13-year-old boy, it seemed to take forever as the men tried to haul the gigantic animal alongside the boat.

They tried to ring the tail. It seemed they were fighting a monster that was still alive, sometimes trying to get away from them and sometimes charging towards them, trying to crush the life out of them. The boat listed from side to side, the wind and sea tossing it like an animal with its prey. The men hauled on the rope, trying desperately to fight the elements at the same time.

The pain in the men's hands was excruciating, and one or two of them were forced to let go. They fell on to the slippery deck in exhaustion. Each time the whale moved away, it nearly took one of the men overboard. Jack watched fascinated as the waves flung icy sea-water down their necks while the boat rocked from side to side.

At length the men managed to get the ring on, and they all collapsed in a heap on the bloodstained deck. They dragged themselves towards the hatchway. The pole fixed in the carcass bent to the wind like a reed. Flakes of snow were whirling through the icy air. Jack wore a thick jersey beneath his oilskin, but still he felt the icy pressure of the wind.

The whale was now cast adrift, and the Captain returned to the bridge.

"Three-quarter speed ahead!" he said.

"Steer for the middle of that iceberg ahead!"

About an hour later the waves had ceased their violent buffeting of the ship, although there was still a heavy swell. The wind had died down a little and was no longer roaring in the rigging. The ship's engines, revolving very slowly, were holding her steady, bows on to the wind and quite unflurried, some 30 metres from a huge iceberg, directly ahead. On each side of the iceberg enormous waves were racing, but under its massive shelf of ice, there lay a calm stretch of water. It would be a refuge for the *Larsen*.

It seemed ironic to the young Jack that a dangerous and lethal seaman's enemy like an iceberg should provide the shelter they needed, and in so doing, become their guardian in the Antarctic.

Although the worst of the storm was over, the *Larsen* sheltered beneath the iceberg for the next 48 hours. There was nothing for the crew to do but remain on board, sleep as long as they liked, and wait for the storm to end. They played cards, listened to music, read books, and generally relaxed. When he was not busy in the galley, Jack lay on his bed thinking about his life in New Zealand. Colac Bay seemed so far away. He was in the middle of a storm, 15 degrees off the South Pole and sheltering under an iceberg! What a tale to tell his mates when he got back!

Up on the deck of the floating factory, snowflakes whirled and the wind howled. The winchmen were bent double, their shoulders hunched, and their gloved hands under their armpits, whenever possible. Steel pincers, slung from one cable and secured by another, looked like a gigantic crab as they sidled towards the afterpart of the vessel, a metre or two above the deck. Two men in seaboots, roped together like mountaineers, brought up the rear. They made for a "tunnel" – a passage cut through the stern of all floating factories and used to haul the carcasses of whales on deck. As soon as the pincers reached the entrance of the tunnel they dipped, settling on the inclined plane of the slipway. One man detached the vertical cable. The steel crab began gliding and crawling towards its prey.

The roped men went down the slope of the tunnel, as if on to a skating-rink, guiding the pincers. Waves lapped against the lower end of the slipway, beyond which showed the tail of the enormous whale. As soon as the pincers came in contact with the tail, one of the roped men turned around, raising his arm to let the other men know. Another man worked the lever, the cable stiffened, and the pincers gripped the base of the tail. The massive whale, weighing 130 tonnes and filling two-thirds of the width of the slipway, started gliding upwards. The whale rose upwards and as it did so, a sheet of saltwater was squirted over it by a hose.

As the whale hit the deck three men armed with long-handled knives proceeded to make incisions on each side of the body. Steel hooks, a yard long, were attached to steel cables. The men plunged the hooks into the blubber near the head.

The whale is hunted for its blubber, its meat, its bones, intestines and vital organs which are cut up and boiled to make oil. A whale's epidermis consists of a very thin elastic cuticle, as transparent as cellophane. The skin immediately beneath is flexible and black, some millimetres thick. Below it again, is a layer of blubber, which may be a foot or more thick. It is the colour of ivory.

The whale lay stretched out on the deck as the cutters began dividing it into big cubes of equal dimensions. The men worked frantically, without pausing for breath. Theirs was a race against the elements. The icy wind covered the men with fine particles of snow. Steam now rose from the freshly sliced blubber.

Sliding about over the blubber, the men were lucky if they didn't cut off one of their own toes as they manipulated their razor-sharp knives. Occasionally one of them would fall on to the carcass and then into the water. He would have to be hauled out of the freezing water and hurried below deck to get warm before hypothermia set in.

Jack watched the men as they sliced the strips of flesh and fat into smaller pieces. These would be melted down in the brick-built furnace, which was stoked first with wood and later with animal refuse. The cutting-up and boiling on deck continued day and night for over two days, with the weary men floundering about in blood and fat, a sickening stench in their nostrils.

Besides Jack there were three other New Zealanders on the ship who helped with the labouring. As the days were long and the work hard, it was a tough life for a young teenage boy. Jack found the scenes of butchery repugnant, and was pleased that his duties were confined to below deck in the galley. He had a very good idea what life would be like for him had he been employed in another capacity on the *Larsen*. He had witnessed much on the whaler – hellish scenes of butchery, driving snow, he had smelled the foul odour of the whole whaling process among the noise and clatter of bone-saws, winches, and he had felt some of the terrible strain imposed on the men. Looking back, he wonders how he survived all those months at sea in those freezing conditions. It was just as well that the *Larsen* weathered the storms and did not collide with an iceberg, because nobody on the ship had been trained in the event of an emergency. It would have been every man for himself, and a small boy like Jack could not possibly have survived.

Finally it was time to leave the *Larsen*. More than nine months had passed, and in all that time Jack had never left the confines of the ship. He wondered how he would cope with ordinary life again. Returning to Stewart Island and the safe harbour of Paterson Inlet, the *Larsen* hit some rocks, putting a large hole in the side of the ship. When they anchored at the Inlet the hole was filled with wooden blocks to enable the ship to return to Norway. For the nine months or so that Jack had been on the ship he received the sum of 381 pounds – a small fortune in those days.

The whaling season had come to an end, and Jack had to adjust to ordinary life again. He was briefly reunited with his parents, who were pleased to see him. But the experience of life at sea had made him realise that he could no longer stay in the tiny Colac Bay settlement, and it was not long before he was on the move once more. This time he left with the blessing of his parents.

Jack wanted to see as much of New Zealand as possible, and he also wanted to see more of life by working in a variety of jobs. He had made a friend of Jimmy Burnett. Jimmy's father owned Half-Way Bay sheep station, and the two boys went to Central Otago to find work.

Their first job was shepherding on a farm at Lake Wakatipu. The farm was situated in the high country, and Jack soon grew to love farm life and appreciate the breathtaking beauty of their surroundings. It was not long before he was learning to muster the sheep. He was a keen worker and learned fast. The sheep were loaded at Kingston and unloaded at Half-Way Bay. Jack was becoming much stronger and fitter physically. He was growing fast, and whenever he was given some time off from farmlife, he would play all types of sport. He was particularly good at rugby and boxing, and would spend nearly all of his free time in these sports.

The following year when Jack was 16, he and Jimmy found more work – this time on a sheep farm near Arrowtown, not far from Lake Hayes. Life on the farm was tough, but he was paid 10/- a week, which wasn't a bad wage for those times. The hours were long and he found it difficult to get used to the harsh, freezing conditions. However, Jack was keen to learn as much as possible about farming. He cut gorse, helped to build a sheep dip, and learned all aspects of farming by watching and working with the other men. He was fast becoming a jack-of-all-trades. On cold winter nights he would stay indoors reading any book he could find. This became his favourite form of relaxation.

He enjoyed mustering perhaps more than anything. His day would start about 2.30am, when he would get out of bed in the early morning chill and join the rest of the musterers for a huge breakfast in the homestead kitchen. They would then go outside in the freezing air to pack their equipment for the day's muster. Jack can still remember quite vividly the sight of The Remarkables mountains looming above him, large, cold and dark as they set off with the sheep dogs barking impatiently around them.

He found the fresh pure mountain air invigorating, and as he glanced up at the mountains, he thought that they had the appearance of crisp folds of crumpled white cloth with icing sugar scattered all over them.

Sometimes the men could be mustering away from the homestead for two or three weeks at a time as the farm was vast and there was much ground to cover. There were no tractors or four-wheel-drive vehicles in those days to help. The sheep had to be brought off the mountains and down to the lower safer pastures well before winter set in.

Very little grew on that stark and barren land except for patches of manuka, gorse and tussock. A few deer, wild pigs and chamois grazed on the odd patch of fertile land, and sometimes Jack would see flocks of black and white Canada geese rise from scrubby matagouri bushes, their giant wings in perfect unison as they flew off in search of grass or clover, the birds' main feed.

"They were such a beautiful sight," says Jack, delight and obvious love for the land etched on his face.

Sometimes, while the other musterers were dozing or taking a rest, he would just stand looking out over the vast expanse of land, deep in thought. Probably that was the only time in his life that he was to experience a euphoria so deep, and unmatched by anything else in his life before or since.

But farmlife was coming to an end, and he felt the need, as always, to move on. His sense of adventure was such that he wanted to see the world, but first he must see the rest of the South Island.

Around this time Jack, who had been practising his boxing at every opportunity, entered a tournament and won his match. This was great for his self-esteem, and he went on to win more matches, eventually winning the Tokanui Cup at the Invercargill Boxing School. He was a lightweight, and fought Jack Kelly, Ray Nicholl, and George McEwen – all light heavyweights. He was paid a pound a trial.

He also ran the half-mile. He represented Tuatapere, Otautau, Tokanui, Inangahua, Reefton and Westland. He was paid eight pounds a race. A keen rugby player, he also played for Hokitika as a fullback.

New Zealanders were taking a great interest in sport, with

rugby and boxing the most popular. The name on everybody's lips in those days was Tom Heeney, the heavyweight boxer from Gisborne. In 1928 Heeney arrived back in New Zealand to a hero's welcome. He had just lost the world championship on a technical knockout.

At the end of the 1920s, and indeed all over the world, New Zealand was a country wracked by severe economic, political and social anguish. The Great Depression was just starting, yet New Zealanders were still struggling to heal the wounds of World War I. People had a sense of hopelessness and bitterness. Their spirits had been crushed and their dreams were broken. They needed something to lift them out of their misery, and to create for them a positive future. At that stage they had no warning that they would need all the strength and resilience to help them to cope with the tumultuous years which lay ahead. They were not to know that within ten years they would be in the midst of another world war.

As jobs were scarce, Jack took any work that was going. He picked raspberries at Waimate for 4/- a day, then he hitched a ride over to the West Coast, and was lucky to get a job helping to put the railway through to Westport. It was 1930 and most single men carried the swag looking for work.

"Everybody was in the same boat," said Jack. "You had to just keep walking."

There were many swaggers around the South Island. They were mainly men who were out of work, completely penniless, and who very often had to depend on the generosity of a farmer's wife for their bread and butter. They roamed the countryside looking for the odd job, and carried all their possessions in a cloth bag, known as a swag. The swag was usually tied to their backs.

"There were so many interesting swaggers around in those days," says Jack. "I particularly remember one interesting character called John the Baptist, also known as 'Mouth-organ Johnny.' As the name suggests, he would often play the mouth-organ, hoping to make a sixpence or two. He was always on the scrounge for a good feed, but when he was given money, he was inclined to go straight on the booze."

John the Baptist was thought to have been killed in Christchurch during World War II.

"I see them now," says Jack, "going up the road with their smoke-blackened billy, pot, and bedroll. Sometimes one would have only one gumboot on, his other foot would perhaps be tied up with string and stocking. Imagine the freezing Canterbury winters, to say nothing of an Otago frost, that those poor unfortunates had to put up with. They would frequently be cold, hungry, wet or sick."

Jack carried his swag to Motueka, Nelson, Blenheim, and on to Ashburton meeting many other swaggers and becoming friendly with them.

About this time Jack decided to try his hand at black-sanding for gold. In those days men were keen to make their fortunes from gold, but it was extremely hard work with little return. Jack had little choice as there was no other work offering.

Jack decided to try his luck at Barrytown, a small farming town about 29 kilometres north of Greymouth. Ever since the 1860s Barrytown had been an important gold-dredging centre in New Zealand. The Barrytown goldfield reached its peak in 1879, and to the diggers it was known as Seventeen Mile (17 miles from the Grey). Officially it was first known as Fosberry, then Barryville, and finally Barrytown. It had 11 hotels and a population of around 2,000 miners. Its gold was beach gold, coarser than most, and probably derived from the creeks to the south including the Ten Mile.

Jack had heard many stories about the gold days in New Zealand. He had been told that the early diggers believed that the gold on the West Coast beaches had been blown over from Australia,

"It's all fine gold, fine as dust," they said. "The heavy stuff stayed in Australia."

Experts have little doubt that the fine gold and its accompanying black sand came down the rivers and was carried northwards by the seadrift to be deposited on the beaches. Jack had to work between the tides in order to retrieve the gold, quite often right through the night. He had a long-handled shovel and gold-pan. He took one or two shovelfuls of dirt and mixed these with plenty of water in the pan. Then he swirled these about to break up any clay lumps, and any larger pebbles or rocks he picked out by hand. He sat at the edge of the stream where the flowing water washed away the mud. He held the pan by the rim at each side and swung it with a short circular motion so that most of the sand and gravel started to lift and move about a little. It was essential that the dirt be lifted and moved in the pan at an early stage, so that the heavy gold and black sand worked to the bottom. He held the pan slightly tilted so that the farther rim just dipped into the stream. He kept the dirt moving, and at the same time dipped the rim in time with the circular motion, so that fresh water swilled in and out. Each time that it swilled out, it carried away some of the tumbling pebbles and half-suspended black sand. Every now and again he lifted the pan and swirled the dirt to spread it back over the bottom. That was to make sure the heavy minerals moved down to the bottom again. As the volume of light sand diminished, the dark streaks of black sand appeared around the edges of the light. When Jack saw the grains of black sand going over the rim, he lifted the pan and gently shook the concentrates back over the bottom.

The black sand was a mixture of the heavy black grains of two minerals – magnetite and ilmenite. This always remained at the bottom of the pan. When the quantity was down to a few spoonfuls, Jack would swirl it around very gently with a slow rolling action, using only half a cupful of water in the pan. This would form a "tail" around the edge of the bottom with the light sand going ahead, the black sand following, and behind that the gold flakes forming the point of the tail.

He had to learn to resist the temptation to touch the colours, unless he had a nugget, because traces of skin oil coating the flakes could make the finer ones float out of the pan when he added water.

If he had a well-separated group of colours in the tail, he would pick them out with the clean blade of a pocket knife and drop them into a small bottle filled with water by dipping the blade. Sometimes, as he became more experienced, he could pan out the black sand, but it took trial and error, skill and patience, and he found generally that most colours are better picked out by hand.

The West Coast was once described as "a very wild place with queer dreadful men about". But most of the diggers were not nearly as dreadful as they no doubt appeared. In the early days of the Goldrush around 1866, they certainly looked rough. They wore high or low-crowned wide-brimmed hats, any old jacket, yellowing clay-stained moleskin trousers and heavy boots. They wore their hair and beards long, which was the fashion in those days. This helped to discourage the sandflies, which were prevalent around Barrytown. Jack wished he could wear his hair long as well, as the sandflies were a curse when he was black-sanding.

Some people made a good living black-sanding at Barrytown as fine gold in those days was 2 pounds 12 shillings and 6 pence a fine ounce. Pure gold, also known as Roddy nugget, was a real find but very rare. In the eighteen months or so that Jack panned for gold he earned small amounts of money, just enough to live on, and then decided to move on once more.

New Zealand, besides being a country wracked by severe economic depression, was also in the middle of an era of great social and political change. Confusion abounded in the 1920s. People were marrying younger, divorcing more often, and had fewer children, even though Plunket now supervised their upbringing. Young women were wearing cosmetics and smoking cigarettes, while others swore. The bra became fashionable. It was also fashionable to discuss Freud and sex. At Otago University the University Council attempted to outlaw the tango at all functions within its jurisdiction, but an outraged student body refused to comply. It seemed to many that the prostitution and larrikinism which were prevalent in the latter part of the 19th century had been replaced by a new and radical social change which created a division between generations. Throughout the 1920s moral debates raged throughout the country. American films, a source of great delight for the younger generation, and new dances evoked images of chaos and anarchy. The 1920s were an era of confusion, ambivalence and uncertainty.

It was in this era of change and confusion that Jack grew from a teenager into a young man. He was busy trying to earn a living, but whenever he could, he would attend a local dance or some other social occasion. In those days the men, young and old, tended to congregate at the end of the hall, mostly out of shyness, and the girls sat in a state of constant fear that they would not be asked for a dance. Jack soon learned the dances of the time – the waltzes, maxinas and the Gay Gordons.

After Jack had moved on from Barrytown he got a temporary job in a sawmill near Lyell, west of Murchison in the Buller Gorge. Lyell, which was named after the British scientist Sir Charles Lyell, was described in a Thomas Cook's travel guide as "a most remarkably situated township, consisting of one curved street cut out of the hillside." Along this street, Main Street, and perched on the hillside above it, there were at various times at least seven stores, five hotels, two churches, a brewery, a court-house, a newspaper office, a school, a bank, a post office, police station, various mining offices, and a number of dwellings. Newman Brothers ran a coach service from Westport, having in 1884 taken over the contract from Job Lines, the pioneer of transport in the Lower Buller, and the man who had brought the first mail to Lyell on horseback in the early 1870s. A Cobb-type coach, also run by Newmans, brought passengers from Nelson and Hampden from 1882 onwards.

The owners of the sawmill in Lyell gave Jack shelter and food but no pay as they were broke. This didn't worry Jack as he was happy just to work. At least he had a roof over his head, and a hot meal at night. Two months later a job bagging coal and carrying it house to house in Otautau, Southland, paid him one pound a week plus his keep. He slept in a bunk in the owner's garage.

What kept him going during those hard days of the Depression? The winters were long and tough, food was always scarce, and he never knew what would happen when his money ran out. He had already gone through much in his young life. What more could there be? He had even experienced the horrors of a serious earthquake. In 1929 he had been living just outside Murchison when the earthquake struck.

"There was a sudden deathly stillness in the air," says Jack today, "and then suddenly I heard a strange rumbling noise. All the animals ran for shelter, and almost at the same time the chimneys and houses started to fall down. I was very frightened. After the main shakes, there were many smaller ones for several days after. I believe some people died in that earthquake."

The earthquake blocked the river and ruined the port of Karamea for some time.

Although New Zealand was in the midst of a depression, one thing lifted its spirits, and that was the "wireless". Radio had begun in New Zealand as far back as 1921 with a broadcast from Otago University by a gifted physicist – Professor Robert Jack. It transformed New Zealand life. Jack can still remember sitting around a farmhouse kitchen listening to the voices and the music of early broadcasts with a mixture of wonder and excitement.

–3–
THE DECADE BEFORE THE WAR

"THE TOWN IS A MAN'S WORLD, BUT THE
COUNTRY LIFE IS OF GOD."
– COWPER –

In 1931 a hero had found its way into the lives of New Zealanders. It was a horse, Phar Lap, nicknamed "Big Red". According to *The Weekly News* at that time, Phar Lap had been bought for 160 guineas, and won more than 66,000 pounds in an age of high competition and low stakes.

In this new age of horse racing in New Zealand, Jack was one of many who were caught up with racing fever. When a job in the local paper to work with trotting horses caught his eye, he immediately borrowed a push bike and rode to the stables. The owner was Jim McConnell and he took to Jack at first sight. Jim was a real character. He came from Northern Ireland and was very superstitious. He had a fear of burglars, and consequently, everything was kept under lock and key.

Jack was paid 25/- a week – a fortune in those days – helping with the horses, feeding them, and occasionally training them. He loved every minute of it. He discovered he had an affinity with animals, an affinity which was to last throughout his life.

Together with Jim, he trained "Vocation", "Blue Prince", "Desert Cloud", and "18 Carat" to name a few. They raced mainly at Gore, Otautau and Wyndham. Jack would feed the horses in the mornings after they had been worked, and then at night about 5.00pm. At first the horses could not win any races, and Jack wondered if perhaps they weren't getting enough to eat. Jim kept the stables locked up and Jack had no idea where he kept the keys. He knew they must be somewhere, so he hunted around and eventually found them. The next morning he gave the horses extra feed, and it had the desired result. The horses started to win races!

Jim was puzzled as to why this was so. One day he said to Jack, It's odd about the feed – it's not lasting like it used to."

Jack replied: "Well, don't look at me. You have the key to the stables!"

After the war Jack told Jim the full story, and they had a good laugh. Jim McConnell lived until well into his 90s, and died at Timaru.

Jack stayed with Jim for about two years, and then worked a short time as a builder's labourer before wandering back over to the West Coast again. He loved the coast and had made many friends there. One of them, Jim O'Brien, the M.P., found him a job with the Public Works. His job was to help build a bridge across the Buller River, and his first boss was George Hawes. Straight away he saw the potential in Jack. He sensed him to be honest, a hard worker with a sense of integrity, and very soon he was made a foreman.

The job with the Public Works entailed travelling around the West Coast, and in the course of his travels and work, Jack met many interesting characters.

One day a group of men arrived from Wellington. Their names were Glad, Sadd, Bright and Wright! When Jack met Harry Bright he was dressed in full tails, spats, and a stiff-fronted shirt. All the time Jack knew him he was immaculately dressed. Bright was a well-educated man, and had been a barrister and a remittance man in England before moving to New Zealand.

When Jack asked him his name, he replied: "Bright, old bean, what!"

The men were given a pick and shovel, a wheelbarrow, hay for mattresses for their tents, and a ball of string. Harry Bright made two friends, Taffy Davis and Tom McGee. They would make home brew and drink it out of milk tins.

With the country still in the midst of the Depression, Jack, together with Harry Bright, Taffy Davis, and Tom McGee, transferred to a place called Kopara, south of Nelson Creek. They helped to open a road to Nelson Creek – not an easy job as the road had to be made from a muddy track made much worse in winter. As Jack was foreman, he now wore a collar and tie.

Harry Bright and his mates had no idea how to fell a tree. Jack would look on fascinated as he watched them scarp it right around rather than putting a front scarp into it. He asked Harry, "Which way is the tree going to fall?"

To which Harry replied, "Good God, man. I'm not a bleeding prophet, what!" Bright was a man full of humour, intelligent, scrupulously honest, and also a voracious reader.

Jack looks back on those days with nostalgia. Although the work was hard, the days were long, and money was short, he met many interesting characters, some of whom became life-long friends. A few years later he met up with some of them again when he entered Burnham Camp at the beginning of the war.

There is a sad footnote to the story of Harry Bright. After Jack took leave of him, Bright became a road surfaceman, filling pot-holes. He was always a heavy drinker, and one night he must have drunk more than usual, because he set fire to his hut in the Fox Glacier and was burned to death.

This was the age of aviation. People found it fascinating, and the excitement and adventure surrounding this new sport helped to lift people's spirits out of the doldrums. One of the most famous aviation heroes of the decade was Charles Kingsford-Smith, an Australian. He was a super-hero to everybody, and he flew hundreds of New Zealanders in his three-engined Fokker mono-plane "Southern Cross". One of his passengers was Jack Hinton. A ride in Kingsford-Smith's plane cost Jack 10/-.

Jack also came into contact with the aviator Guy Menzies. In January 1931 Menzies completed the first solo flight across the Tasman Sea to Harihari on the West Coast of the South Island. Harihari was originally known as Hende's Ferry. The town made world headlines when Menzies crash-landed his Avro-Avian air-craft "Southern Cross Junior" in the La Fontaine swamp, seven kilometres from the little settlement. He had been refused permission to make the flight and said he was flying from Sydney to Perth. However, instead of heading westwards he flew east to

New Zealand. His personal luggage during the 11-hour trip contained a razor, a toothbrush and a spare collar. Thunderstorms over the Tasman threw the tiny single-seater plane about, sometimes from five metres above the stormy sea to 3,350 metres up in the clouds.

Menzies had set off from Sydney for New Plymouth but he had to do a forced landing outside the town in the swamp behind a homestead at Harihari.

Jack happened to be in Harihari when Menzies landed his plane. Menzies told people later that he wouldn't tackle the flight again "unless someone gave me five thousand quid!"

Jack was in need of urgent medical treatment in the same year. One day chopping firewood in a hurry he accidentally chopped his thumb almost completely off. Somehow he managed to wrap a piece of rag around it, and two of his friends drove him to find a doctor. The only doctor they were able to find was very intoxicated. He told Jack he might be able to save the thumb, but unfortunately he had no anaesthetics. He gave him a couple of brandies and told Jack to hope for the best while he sewed up the thumb. Amazingly, the surgery was successful, and Jack has not had any trouble with the thumb since.

Jack was working 48 hours a week. There was always something to do. In the evening he did his washing and cleaning up, and on Sundays he and his friends played rugby – he was secretary of the local rugby club. Some of the men he worked with and socialised with were to become household names – men like Stan Whitehead who finished up as Speaker of the House for the Labour Government, and Bob Semple, Minister of Works in Michael Savage's Labour Government.

It was Bob Semple, a former Australian miner, and according to journalist Pat Booth "easily the most colourful political speaker of his generation, perhaps of any New Zealand era", who once talked of workers "wiping the sweat from their brows with the slack of their bellies".

Jack and his friends at the Ministry of Works were all working for about 8/- a day. However, their pay was relative to the cost of living. A set of dungarees, a jacket, and a pair of trousers cost

44

about three pounds ten shillings.

Jack had two camp ovens and cooked everything in them. Food was very cheap and he could cook beautiful meals.

One night, not long after the mishap with his thumb, Jack was asleep in his hut when he was awakened by a fellow called Tom who suffered from what would be termed today as chronic depression. Then he was looked on as weird, or slightly loopy. Tom grabbed Jack and shook him awake.

"I'm either going to kill myself, or kill someone else," he shouted to Jack.

"For Christ's sake, don't kill me!" said Jack in a panic. He took him to Seaview Mental Hospital, but they discharged him and Tom went back to his job on the road site.

One night shortly after this incident, Jack went to check on the working gangs but was unable to find Tom. He and the men searched everywhere, and finally found him. He was lying in a stream, having slit his throat and cut both his wrists. Jack rang the police at Ross and the local parish priest, Father Brown. Almost immediately, the police rang Jack back. Could Jack lay old Tom out? Of course he had no option but to do as he was asked, so he had a couple of whiskies and tied the body down with some flax. By this time he was exhausted, so he sat down in a chair to wait for the priest. His eyes closed for what seemed to be only a few minutes, when he woke suddenly with a start. He felt sure a noise had woken him, and he looked in the direction of where he thought it could have come from. What he saw made him jump nearly out of his skin. In the half-light of the dawn filtering through the window he saw Tom raise his arms in the air, one after the other. Just as he was running out of the door in fright, he realised what must be happening. It was a most unusual type of rigor mortis.

After the miserable years of the Depression, New Zealanders started to enjoy themselves. They could dance all night for the price of a shilling or two to the sounds of Tommy Dorsey, Duke Ellington, Count Basie and all the other big bands. It was all finally over and it was time for singing and dancing. No truer words were spoken than the song "Life Is Just A Bowl Of

Cherries" which was on everybody's lips. New Zealanders were also able to lose themselves in the fantasies they saw depicted on the big screen.

In 1935 the economy took a turn for the better. Michael Joseph Savage, or Mickey Savage, as he was affectionately known to thousands of New Zealanders, became the country's first Labour Prime Minister. His dream of a socialist New Zealand not only brought the country out of the nightmare of the Depression, but he made several fundamental changes, one of which was the introduction of the 40-hour week, or the five-day working week. The lives of the workers changed for the better. For the first time in his life Jack no longer had to work on a Saturday.

Whole new suburbs around the country were developed and roads were built. Even some of the Cabinet ministers, including Bob Semple, in their shirt sleeves and waistcoats, helped in the building of some of these homes.

With all the work that Jack had been doing over the years, together with his great interest in sport, there had not been a great deal of time for meeting, and becoming involved with, women. However, that was soon to change. In 1927 he had met Eunice Henriksen. She was married to a man of Norwegian descent, and she and her husband Alfred were involved in trotting. They owned the Santa Rosa Stud in Halswell just out of Christchurch, and for a short time Jack had worked on their stud farm.

In 1936 he met her again in Kumara on the West Coast. Her marriage to Alfred had broken down, and she was working in the Dundalk Hotel owned by her parents. Although she was 12 years older than Jack they got along extremely well. They had much in common. Eunice, or Eunie, as Jack called her, was kind and thoughtful, with dark hair and laughing brown eyes and a personality to match. Very popular, she got on with everybody. She was a Catholic, and when her friendship with Jack developed into something stronger, her strong religious beliefs prevented her from remarrying until Alfred died. Jack loved her very much. As one of Jack's friends says: "It was difficult not to love Eunie. She was a wonderful person."

In 1937 Eunie bought the lease for the Hari Hari Hotel in

Westland. Jack had managed to save some money and he put this into the pub with Eunie.

Doug Eggelton, who now lives in Christchurch, was a good friend of Jack when they were both working for the Public Works on the West Coast. They still meet today and reminisce.

"My first impression of Jack was that he was a bit of a dare-devil," he says, "but whatever he said, he meant. You always knew where you were with him – he was a real straight-shooter. He was great company, and always willing to help anybody. He was the driver, and I was the mechanic repairing the tractors and machinery. Jack drove the first D8 Bulldozer Caterpillar diesel, and we operated mainly from Jacob's River, South Westland. The men had a great respect for Jack, and he was well-liked."

Doug worked with Jack for about four years at the Ministry of Works, their job often taking them from Otira to Franz Josef and the Fox Glaciers.

"I can remember once going to Otira with Jack and calling into the pub there. The publican must have been pretty impressed with Jack because he asked him if he could take over the hotel as he had to go to Christchurch to make arrangements for some more beer. Jack enjoyed taking over the pub and looking after the customers. He was a natural as a publican."

By the latter part of the 1930s Jack had worked on the construction of many roads on the West Coast. The roads had often been built through heavy bush and swamp country, making the job a difficult one. A few years later, after Jack had won the Victoria Cross, a friend of his who had worked with him on some of these jobs was interviewed by the *Christchurch Press*.

"I knew Jack fairly well," said the soldier, "and I also knew some of the men on the job. They all said he was one of the best bosses they had worked for. He was a very quiet type, but was well known and popular on the Coast. Jack was the kind who would take off his coat and work with the men. Sometimes, when I arrived out at the Hari Hari camp with supplies, I could see one of the men just doing odd jobs about the camp. It usually turned out that he had been feeling a bit crook and Jack had found some light work for him to do. That's the kind he was.

"I remember one day when I arrived and he was in camp doing his books. He asked me to stay for lunch – he never let anyone go away without a meal or a cup of tea. Well, after dinner, Jack said he was going out to catch a few whitebait. Just something fresh for the boys' tea, he said."

The 1930s were drawing to a close and the darkening shadows of war over Europe were beginning to spread to New Zealand. It should have been a time of joy and relaxation. New Zealand was about to celebrate its first centenary and, according to some people, it now had perhaps the highest standard of living in the world. It should have been a great start to the next century. However, as playwright Bruce Mason was soon to write, it was "the end of the golden weather".

–4–
THE BIGGEST ADVENTURE OF
THEIR LIVES

"WARS, AND RUMOURS OF WAR"
– MATTHEW XXIV. 6 –

For New Zealanders who had been filled with a sense of hope after Mickey Savage's government had won its second victory in 1938, those feelings were replaced by uncertainty. Savage's first Labour Government of 1935 had promised them an age of economic and social reform, and there was no reason to believe that this would not happen. Subsequently, people felt their lives would now change for the better.

In 1938 when Labour took 56 per cent of the vote, it was the first time in 30 years that a Government had gained more votes than all the opposing parties put together. It was no wonder that New Zealand was bathed in a golden glow. Mickey Savage, New Zealand's new hero, was kind, gentle and caring, and a most powerful politician. He was the first New Zealander to sway the new country so completely. His reign was not to be a long one, but he would remain forever in the hearts of the people.

He had a memorable speech characteristic. He would preface his speeches with the words: "Now then", and excited Kiwis would rise to their feet in a fit of excitement. His photo gazed down from the walls of thousands of New Zealand homes. Writer Pat Booth refers to him as "a modern-day Moses leading his chosen people from the wilderness to the Promised Land". John A. Lee, himself a controversial figure and hero to some in the 1930s, wrote that Savage told him: "The people think that I am God."

They did too; he was the answer to their prayers, and he could do no wrong. It was partly this sense of hero-worship that made so many young New Zealand men follow unquestionably Savage's plea to enlist when World War II was declared in 1939. It certainly helped to sway Jack and his friends to join up – not that they needed much swaying. For a long time Jack had been incensed by Hitler's aggression.

Rumblings of war had been heard as far back as 1936 when Adolf Hitler and Benito Mussolini, Fascist dictator of Italy, supported General Francisco Franco, a rebel officer, in an armed revolt against the Spanish Government. This led to a civil war which raged throughout Spain for almost three years. The three dictators, Hitler, Mussolini and Franco, used this war as a chance to test out their armaments, thus staging a dress rehearsal for total war. Franco was victorious, later becoming dictator of Spain in 1939.

In that same year, Hitler and Mussolini became military and political allies when they signed what they called "a Pact of Steel" – an alliance which committed one partner to help the other should he be involved in a war.

The rest of the world looked on helplessly as Hitler took Austria in 1938 in just a few days. Later in the same year he annexed the Sudetenland – a part of Czechoslovakia. At this point Neville Chamberlain, Prime Minister of Great Britain, flew to Germany in an attempt to stop Hitler. On September 29, 1938 Chamberlain, French Premier Edouard Daladier, Hitler and Mussolini signed the Munich Agreement which dismembered Czechoslovakia. Chamberlain returned to London triumphantly waving the so-called "Peace Agreement" – "peace in our time" he called it. It wasn't worth the paper it was written on.

There was an uneasy quiet for a little less than a year until, predictably, Hitler ignored the Peace Treaty and marched into Czechoslovakia. The rest of the world watched in helpless resignation as Hitler took that country without a single shot being fired.

In August 1939, after Great Britain and France announced that they would guarantee Poland's frontiers, promising to go to war if Germany attacked, the Nazi forces struck at Poland.

On 1 September, the British Government advised the German

Government that unless it could give satisfactory assurances that Germany had suspended all aggressive action against Poland, Britain would, without hesitation, fulfil its obligations towards Poland. No such assurances were received, and accordingly a state of war existed between Great Britain and Germany as from 11.00am British summer time, 3 September, 1939.

In New Zealand on that fateful Sunday at precisely 11.45pm a telegram was received by the Governor-General which said simply: "War has broken out with Germany". Within a few hours a *New Zealand Gazette* Extraordinary declared that a state of war existed between New Zealand and the German Reich as from 9.30pm 3 September, New Zealand standard time.

World War II had begun. The New Zealand Government concurred entirely with Britain's actions and led the nation into a new world war alongside Britain. It seems ironic today, that two of its members, Bob Semple and Peter Fraser, had gone to prison for opposing military service in World War I. On that fateful night after 9.30pm the news soon spread throughout the country.

Jack was in Greymouth with Eunie when he heard the news over the radio. As he listened to Savage's words: "Where Britain goes, we go", he determined that he would enlist as soon as volunteers were called for. Savage was strongly behind Britain, the Mother Country as he called it, and he announced that his Government would seek voluntary enlistment from young men of military age for the three services. Enlistment offices would open at 9.00am on Tuesday, September 12th.

Patriotism and a sense of duty was extraordinarily strong and widespread in almost every town in New Zealand. The majority of young New Zealanders were saying: "Let's get into this thing and get it cleaned up". Volunteers reached nearly 60,000 before conscription was introduced, and 306,000 New Zealanders over the next five years were to be called up either for service at home or abroad.

Jack was one of the enthusiastic Kiwis who joined up in a hurry. He was in a hurry because he thought, as so many of his mates did, that Hitler was bluffing, and that the war would be over before he could get in and fight. About twenty of Jack's friends went down to the recruiting office in Greymouth with him to sign up. Around this time he had a telegram from his father to "do his duty". He also had a small package from his father enclosing three stripes from his father's service in the Boer War. A note said: "Here – sew these on!"

Eunie knew that Jack would enlist. She tried to reason with him to wait a while. The war might soon be over, she told him. Why put his life in danger unnecessarily? She needed him here, with her. He was 30 years of age. Let the younger ones go, she said.

As much as Eunie tried to dissuade Jack from going, he remained adamant that he had no choice. He was determined that he was going to get in there with the best of them and get the whole mess cleaned up as quickly as possible. He loved Eunie deeply and he knew he would miss her dreadfully, but even those powerful feelings would not shut out the strong sense of justice that he had to help in some way to put an end as quickly as possible to the evils of Nazism.

Jack Hinton was a determined and also a very stubborn man. Once he had made up his mind about something, nothing in the world could change it. Nothing would budge him from choosing a certain path or doing things a certain way, whether it be the right or the wrong way. Eunie was also a determined and strong woman. But she was intelligent enough to know that if she managed to dissuade Jack from going to war, as unlikely as that could be, he would be unhappy and feel that somehow he had opted out, that he had taken a cowardly action, and Jack Hinton was certainly no coward.

Eunie wisely gave up the fight. She loved and respected Jack more than anybody in the world, and so she gave in gracefully. Strangely enough, after she accepted the situation, she found it easier to cope.

On 5 October the first South Island enlistments, which were to become part of the First Echelon, made their way to various railway stations to entrain for Burnham Military Camp, about 25 kilometres from Christchurch. At Greymouth railway station Jack joined a large queue to board the train. All around him he could hear the excited shouts as people greeted each other. In amongst the noise and confusion he saw some of his friends from Westport and the surrounding districts who were on their way to Burnham too.

Once on board the train the noise settled down. It wasn't long before they made up a song. It went something like this:

"We are Mickey Savage's soldiers –
The West Coast infantry.
We cannot fight, we cannot drill,
so what bloody use are we?
We fight for King and country,
and girls we used to know,
and all the other bastards that haven't the guts to go."

On the way over to Burnham Camp they stopped at a tearoom for a cup of tea, and Jack was delighted to find that Jim O'Brien the M.P. was on the train too. The two men had often had a drink together in the "Brine Brew" in Greymouth. O'Brien had gone over to the West Coast from Wellington, and had gone back to Greymouth, his home town. Jack had a particular affinity with Jim O'Brien, and thought he was one of the best along with Bob Semple, Paddy Webb, and Harry Holland. O'Brien was a great card player, and was particularly good at 45s. He would often play with an old fellow in the "Brine Brew", and was also a well-known figure in the Kells Hotel at Cobden. The story goes that Jim O'Brien and Warrior Kells, who owned Kells Hotel, which Eunie and Jack bought together later on, were buried side by side with a bottle of beer and a pack of cards – just so they could play 45s together.

The long train journey from Greymouth to Burnham came to an abrupt end at a plantation of tall bluegum trees. This was Burnham Military Camp. It is recorded in *20 Battalion and Armoured Regiment* by D.J.C. Pringle and W.A. Glue that as the long column of train-weary volunteers, some of them dishevelled and far from sober, trudged past him into camp, their future Commanding Officer remarked to a subaltern standing near him,

"This is going to be the best infantry in the world." These were prophetic words. These men were going to be part of 20 Battalion which was going to collect three Victoria Crosses – the only New Zealand battalion to do so in World War II.

All the men were given a special regimental number – Jack's was 7930, and then given a few beers which went down well as it had been a long hot day. In the end there were quite a few more tipsy than sober. Captain Jim Burrows, a schoolmaster from Christchurch, who was in command of B Company, and who would become one of the 20th's most loved Commanding Officers, recounts in his autobiography *Pathway Among Men* that he was completing a final round of the huts later that night with some of the platoon commanders, when he heard a voice calling for help. They searched and found a man in one of the drainage holes. They helped him out, then he turned around and fell straight back into the hole again. He was enjoying a quiet weep as they helped him out a second time.

The following morning, with most of the men a little the worse for wear, they were formed into companies. This was done on a geographical basis – A Company under Major MacDuff, came from Canterbury, B Company under Captain Burrows, from Southland and C Company under Captain Mathewson, from Nelson, Marlborough and the West Coast, and lastly D Company under Captain Paterson, from Otago.

Jack was in C Company, No. 14 Platoon, and most of the men discovered that they already knew each other. All were under the overall command of Lieutenant-Colonel Howard Kippenberger, a veteran of the World War I. Kippenberger had been a Territorial officer in the years between the wars, and had risen to command 1 Battalion, the Canterbury Regiment. Kippenberger had made an intensive study of military history, and throughout the course of World War II, when he rose to the rank of Major-General, he became known as perhaps one of New Zealand's most dearly loved and respected soldiers.

Kippenberger, a solicitor from Rangiora, would tolerate almost anything from his men, as long as they would be "good soldiers" when the time came. Jim Burrows, who succeeded

Kippenberger as Commanding Officer of the 20th, described him as a man who dedicated himself completely and absolutely to the task ahead.

"He was a true soldier, with the true soldier's regard for his men. I do not think he was ambitious in the sense that personal advancement meant everything. He was ambitious for the battalion, the brigade, the division. He was so absorbed in the personal safety of his men to the exclusion of his own, that his men realised that he thought of them more than himself."

Also in C Company was a 31-year-old land valuer from Christchurch named Charles Hazlitt Upham. Upham, with his distinctive qualities of leadership, resource and initiative, had the same typical qualities as Jack – strength of purpose, stubbornness and determination. As a result of his outstanding bravery and defiance of his own personal miseries amidst the horrors of the war, Charles Upham was to win the Victoria Cross twice – the only combatant in two world wars to win a double V.C.

During the first week the new recruits were initiated into every phase of army life, many of them tedious. For example, it was strange for many to wait in interminable queues for meals, and for medical and dental treatment. Many men found it difficult at first to adjust to the strangeness of it all – shouted commands and the absolute lack of privacy. Jack was able to fit into the new life easier than most, for he had always lived the kind of life where he had to share with others and live with other people.

Jack was soon made a sergeant, as was Charles Upham. In the first five or six weeks training comprised of squad drill, arms drill and weapon training, using the old Lee-Enfield rifle, a relic left over from World War I. Jack learnt how to use a Lewis machine-gun and a bayonet. Nearly all the equipment was inadequate, mostly from World War I. However, as Jack had always had to fend for himself, he used the skills he had learnt during his life to teach the men survival techniques; this expertise taught by an ordinary bloke to ordinary men gave them a heightened sense of security and proved invaluable in the many battles which lay ahead.

Very quickly a team spirit, so vital to morale, was established.

The men respected Jack and learnt much from him. Jack Hinton did not have to ask for respect from his men – it was given automatically. He had a natural ability to command and lead without having to depend on seniority of rank. He did not "talk down" to his men; he talked "with them". The men instinctively knew that whatever action they were in, Jack Hinton would be with them.

South Islander Frank Helm was in the same hut and the same platoon as Jack. He found Jack to be an unassuming man, easy to get along with.

"Although Jack was ten years older than the rest of us, he was always one of us," says Helm. "Even when he was a sergeant, he was still one of the boys. He never looked for promotion. Stripes did not mean that much to him, except it meant that he was responsible for his men. Jack would rather go into the NAAFI canteen and drink with us than go into the Sergeants' Mess. He was also a most generous man and a very good friend. If anybody was ever stuck for a bob or two when they went on leave, Jack would be the first to lend some money."

At Burnham the men did a great deal of route marching. Some of these marches were as long as 30 kilometres. At times they seemed to do little else. They fell in and marched to meals; they marched to sick parade and church parade. After breakfast there was a last-minute rush before platoon parade and the sergeant's inspection and roll call, followed by the platoon officer's inspection. Then the sergeant-major's call for "Markers" and "March on", and a company fall-in.

Battalion parades at Burnham were fussy affairs. The men were repeatedly told by their officers that they instilled pride for the battalion, discipline and smartness. As one 20th man, Bill Glue says: "I still have memories after 50 odd years of the Padre's nautical drill movements and the RSM's nagging when addressing the parade. 'Keep still than man!' seemed to be his constant cry. We often wondered which of the 801 of us in the battalion he was complaining about."

The men were told "Slap the butt of your rifle!" A dour Scot in Bill's platoon, chastened for his lack of enthusiasm was later heard to comment: "Any bloody fool can sl-a-ap his bloody rifle."

When the men were proficient in the handling of all weapons it was decided that they could go on night manoeuvres.

The defending company left camp about midday for the scene of operations, which was usually three or four hours away at Tai Tapu. After a suitable time the attackers would leave, allowing the first party to organise its defence. On one of these exercises at Tai Tapu, the enemy was under some trees across the road, and the only direct way to get to them was to crawl through a culvert. Jack crawled through this culvert and came up just in front of the place where the enemy was attacking. With his rifle he fired a blank cartridge in front of the opposing platoon commander. This caused everybody to let fire in a mad frenzy. Jack was not very popular for some time after that incident.

On 23 November the battalion moved by rail to Cave where more field training was carried out. The men returned to Burnham on 3 December. Flu went around the camp, but Jack fortunately kept well. About the time the men were at Cave, Savage publicly announced that the Special Force, as the First Echelon was known, would shortly go overseas.

After the return to Burnham the men went on final leave. Jack went straight down to Colac Bay to visit his parents. They were delighted to see him again. His mother, Mary, was not at all happy that he was going away to war, and as Eunie had done, tried to dissuade him from going. He spent Christmas with his parents, and when it was time to return to Greymouth and to Eunie, he bade his parents farewell, taking care to let his mother know that he would return.

"I'll see you before long," he told her.

Whilst on leave in Greymouth Jack was one of many who sent telegrams to Fred Jones, Minister of Defence. This was to ask for free rail travel passes without limitations. During World War I soldiers on final leave had been given free rail passes anywhere within New Zealand, but in the early days of World War II, the soldiers were given only a one-way ticket to their homes. Most of the men considered this unfair, and the result was that there were a number of unauthorised telegrams to the Minister of Defence asking for free rail travel 'anywhere'.

Jack was one man who had long decided that if one wanted anything in this life, one had to ask for it. However, Jack's telegram failed to reach Freddie Jones and Jack was given a proper dressing down when he returned to Burnham. No change in arrangements was made, except that individual passes allowed the men more freedom to travel.

Jack made his will, courtesy of the Canterbury Law Society, and a gratuity of three pounds was paid to each man. On 30 December, visitors were allowed into the camp for the last time before the men sailed for overseas. A huge afternoon tea was laid out for the families of the men, who were able to spend precious last moments with their husband, brother, son or lover.

On 3 January 1940 the battalion marched through the streets of Christchurch for an official farewell in Cranmer Square, and on the 5th, 800 strong, marched to Burnham station to entrain for Lyttelton. For the third time in 40 years New Zealand troops were about to go overseas. When the men reached Lyttelton they were amazed to see a large crowd gathered at the wharf. The two trains drew close to the ships *Dunera* and *Sobieski*, a Polish ship. The city of Christchurch had turned out to farewell the men. To the parents of these young men, some leaving home for the first time in their lives, history was repeating itself. Only 25 years ago the fathers of these boys had left home themselves to fight a war they thought would end all wars. Mothers clung tightly to their sons. Would they ever see them again, they wondered? The feelings they had in their hearts must have been overwhelming.

Younger people in the crowd were caught up in the excitement of the moment. It never occurred to a great majority of them that these men might not return. They were off on the greatest adventure of their lives. They were going to see the world, and at the Government's expense! Most of them thought, as Jack did, that the war would be over before they got there.

On the faces of some of the older people there was grim determination – it was essential to keep "a brave face" – and even if the unthinkable happened, what better way to go than to die for one's country?

Brigadier Jim Burrows said later: "Forty years ago we were faced with the fact that a most vicious force was going to conquer the world. Historians point out that there has never been a war where there was so clearly a right and a wrong. We were on the side of the right, but when you are faced with the evils of war you have no option but to get in and fight."

Jack was marshalled with the rest of the 20th into alphabetical order and their names were checked as they walked up the gangway in single file, the last man absent without leave having been dragged from his home and hurried down to the wharf.

It was about 5.00pm when the *Dunera* left the shores of Lyttelton to the strains of "Now is the Hour" and "He Careth For Me". It was the first transport to leave New Zealand in World War II, and would be followed shortly by the *Sobieski*. A comment by the bosun went down on record:

"I've seen soldiers, I've seen sailors, I've seen boy scouts, but I've never seen bastards like these!"

The *Dunera* had carried troops and their families to and from India before the war. Jack stood on the deck and watched the figures on the wharf become smaller and smaller. He was excited, pent-up with the emotions of the long day. He thought of Eunie. It had been a great wrench to leave her, and his mother. Now he was completely on his own. He had taken a gamble, but he would probably get away with it, he reasoned. Field-Marshal Kesselring had said: "War is a rough game", but most men felt that if anybody was going to be killed or hurt it would be somebody else, not them.

In the First Echelon somewhere, somehow, a label was tied to these men. They were said to be wife-beaters, debt-dodgers, and income-tax evaders. In due course this talk seeped through to the men in Egypt. Most of them just laughed and refused to take it seriously, but deep down it hurt all the same. How could it not hurt them? They had volunteered to fight for freedom and the New Zealand way of life; they knew what was expected of them and many paid with their lives.

The *Dunera* sailed up the coast from Lyttelton, joined the rest of the convoy from Wellington, passed through Cook Strait and headed west. The last sight Jack Hinton had of his country was Mt. Egmont, its snow-capped peak glistening in the bronze setting sun.

–5–
DESERT TRAINING

"YE IMMORTAL GODS! WHERE IN THE
WORLD ARE WE?"
– CICERO –

The following day after sailing from New Zealand – 6 January, 1940 – the *Dunera* turned west for Australia. Jack stood on the deck watching patrol planes, flying low over the ships, dipping their wings in salute. This was the beginning of a long voyage to Egypt – destination Maadi Camp.

Jack quickly settled down to life on board the troopship, even though there was very little room to move. The *Dunera* had been adapted to carry the greatest number of people in the smallest possible space. He and the rest of the men were in peak physical condition and excellent spirits. Some had never been on a ship before, but for Jack, it brought back memories of that time, now so long ago, when he had been a young cabin boy on the *C.A. Larsen*. Sometimes, on the rare times when he was alone, he would compare this voyage with the one he had taken in 1922.

The days were always busy with physical training, concerts, lectures, and games. The *Dunera* stopped in Western Australia and the men were given leave, when they visited Perth and the old port of Fremantle.

On 30 January the ship docked in Colombo, where Jack had more leave. This busy port was cluttered with ships from all nations. While the *Dunera* was docked Jack was surrounded by native vendor boats selling fruit, nuts, cheroots and small mementos. Jack joined the rest of the men in throwing coins over the side of the ship, and watched as small boys dived for them.

As the *Dunera* approached its eventful destination, Egypt, the men were lectured on the pitfalls of Egypt, the various tropical diseases they might encounter and its strategic importance. Egypt was in a particularly vital position as it was near the Suez Canal and the Middle East oil supplies.

After a voyage of six weeks Jack arrived at Port Tewfik. It was 12 February, 1940, and 20 Battalion disembarked two days later. They marched from the railway station to Maadi but their first impressions were far from favourable. From as far as the eye could see stretched endless sand and barren land. As it was summer, plagues of flies descended on the men in droves. They stuck to their clothing, their faces, their hair, food and utensils. The heat was oppressive.

There were approximately 6,500 troops in the First Echelon – all in Maadi Camp in tents. Roads were eventually built to the camp, and messes, huts, canteens and other buildings were erected. Everything was covered in a shimmering haze, and to the west beyond the camp the pyramids of Giza stood out amidst the desert haze, rather like a huge, awesome gateway to the limitless desert beyond.

However, Maadi township was an attractive, shady, tree-lined village on the banks of the Nile River. Beautiful gardens and expensive homes lined the river banks.

When Jack drove into Cairo on leave he was fascinated by the fact that he had to drive on the right-hand side of the road. It became quite an art dodging donkey carts, fruit barrows, tram cars and cartloads of Egyptian women (or bints as they were known). This long stretch of road leading out of the camp to Cairo was known as the Mad Mile.

After the long period at sea Jack and the rest of the 20th were quite happy to carry on with their training. New infantry weapons – Brens, mortars and anti-tank rifles – were issued to the men, but unfortunately these were on a small scale and were to be used for training purposes only. There were 2" mortars but no training sights for them, and the rest of the rifles and bayonets were of World War I vintage.

Jack found that far from being homesick, he was caught up in the excitement and the thrill of adventure. Life was now so different from that in New Zealand. The fact that his future was uncertain provided him with even more of an impetus to get to grips with the situation and do something practical for the war effort. Most of the 20th men felt the same way.

Meanwhile, in Europe the winter of 1939-40 was the coldest for over 200 years, and Hitler was forced to postpone his invasion of the west 13 times. The BBC reported the falls of Denmark, Norway, Belgium, Luxembourg, Holland and France.

At home in New Zealand the atmosphere was different. In Wellington the Centennial Exhibition was in full swing. Kiwis forgot, for a little while, their worries about the war in Europe, and joined in the celebrations. The Exhibition seemed to epitomise the feelings of the time – excitement, and adventure tinged with a sadness generated by war.

However, Jack was not enjoying himself at that time. He had been sent to Abbassia to take a course in high explosives. He was a natural choice for this, as during the 1930s he had had some dealing in explosives. While he was at Abbassia part of his job was to select men for explosives tuition. One incident of that time, he relates with sadness:

"One chap I selected had told me he had previous experience, and I had no reason to disbelieve him. It couldn't have been true, because he lost both his eyes to a mine. He was sent home to New Zealand where he later married a nurse."

On a visit to Abbassia, General Bernard Freyberg, commander of 2 NZEF, and World War I V.C. winner, visited C Company 20 Battalion during its field firing practice. Concerned about the men's welfare, he asked the sergeant in charge, Jack Hinton,

"How are the men shooting?"

"How would you expect them to bloody well shoot?" replied Jack briskly, without stopping to think – "Not enough bloody rations, stinking heat and sand."

"Repeat that" said Freyberg. Hinton repeated it.

"What's your name, sergeant?"

"Hinton, sir."

"Oh yes, Hinton," said Freyberg. "Carry on."

Freyberg then had a few words with the company commander, who in turn had a few words with his sergeant on how to speak to generals. However, it is recorded in the 20 Battalion and Armoured Regiment's unit history that a grant of one penny per man per day to buy extra rations had been approved.

It took a while to become accustomed to the desert's strange climate. Jack found the nights surprisingly cold and there was much rain in March. A desert wind, known as the khamsin, similar in many ways to a Canterbury nor'wester – a hot, dry wind – became a curse to the men. When the khamsin blew, it would often flatten tents and once the end wall of the camp cinema was blown down. It would blow into their tents and cover their clothing with sand. Even their food was covered with it. It was extremely hot during the day and there never seemed to be any cure for constant thirst. Then there were the never-ending flies, which caused Gippo tummy, as it was known to the troops. This condition was more prevalent in the summer months.

The men looked forward to leave in Cairo, dirty but exciting, with its cafes and bars, museums, colourful bazaars and stalls, its dirty cinemas, the lure of the Burkha, and shoe-shine boys who would ask the soldiers "You want my sister? She very clean, only 10 piastres."

Back home while the troops were in Egypt, New Zealand went into mourning. Mickey Savage, beloved by all, had died from cancer in April. Never before in New Zealand's history were there such open displays of emotion. In Wellington his body lay in state for two days. Fifty thousand people filed past and then the casket went to Auckland by train, where 200,000 people lined the route to Bastion Point where he was buried. Deputy Leader Peter Fraser took over.

The cinema at Maadi Camp was frequented by all the troops. However, the quality of the films shown was inferior and there were frequent breakdowns. Jack Hinton remembers well the dissatisfaction they all felt. One night events reached crisis point. On this particular night, 26 April, there had been more than the usual number of stoppages, and when the men demanded their money back, and this reasonable request was denied, they proceeded to push the walls down and demolish the cinema.

In New Zealand voluntary enlistment had ceased. There had

been a total of 58,000 volunteers, and there had been a last-minute rush to join up. Next day that reliable newspaper, the *Egyptian Mail* published the fact that 58,000 men had joined up in a last-minute rush!

By May it was evident that Italy would soon enter the war. Accordingly sandbags were erected to shelter anti-aircraft guns. Air defence exercises began. On 10 June Italy declared war on Great Britain. Kiwi troops were delighted. Jack took an active part in the celebrations. He helped to disperse the tents and sandbag them for safety, and dig slit trenches. The pattern of his life had now changed. Officers wore revolvers at all times as it was felt that Italian paratroops might descend on them "any time now". Once a day the men held rehearsals in case of any emergency. Just before dawn, and again at dusk, they moved to action stations with two platoons as perimeter guards and a third as a mobile reserve. However, nothing happened and the men waited in vain.

Cairo had its first air-raid alarm at 2 o'clock in the morning of 22 June, when the city's sirens shrieked and searchlights and tracer shells from Egyptian anti-aircraft batteries lit up the sky. A report that bombs had been dropped proved false.

In July 20 Battalion left Maadi for the Western Desert on its first tour of duty in the Mersa Matruh area. The Western Desert is a huge expanse of red ground, red rocks, and red sand. A torrid wasteland, it extends from the Mediterranean to the Sahara, taking in most of Egypt and Libya. There is no vegetation and there are few living creatures save for a few bird species, like sand grouse, the Saharan eagle owl, vultures and gangas. The camel is the most well-known desert animal but there are also hares, tortoises, gazelles, and the desert rat, not forgetting the flies – the scourge of the desert soldier.

A great compensation to life in the Western Desert was bathing in the warm waters of the Mediterranean. This helped to relieve the awful monotony of army life, especially at this time when nothing was happening. Jack found that bathing helped to lift his spirits. A good proportion of the men were suffering from dysentery caused by plagues of flies. In three weeks 98 men were admitted to a British hospital in Alexandria with this complaint.

The Second Echelon had been diverted to England in May 1940, and to the men in the desert, where life was tedious and dull, it looked as if they had been forgotten. Duties were mainly coast-watching and protecting the airfields.

It was essential to keep their spirits up. On some of the route marches someone would start up a song. The hits of the day were "Roll Out the Barrel" and "We'll Hang Out our Washing on the Siegfried Line" – the latter much-scorned after the fall of France. Best known were the marching songs of the First World War, but they seemed out of place somehow. "It wasn't our war we were singing about", says Bill Glue.

"We used to talk about how good it would be if we had a song of our own, but no one ever tried to write one."

Suddenly out of the blue, the men were ordered back to the Western Desert, to Baggush, and the Australians were left to guard Amiriya.

"Baggush, dear old Baggush by the sea.
You can tell them all,
That we did damn all,
In Baggush by the sea."

Baggush was to be their desert home for the last three months of 1940. An oasis near the Mediterranean coast about 50 kilometres east of Mersa Matruh, Baggush was a piece of sandy, rocky desert on which the men built a defensive "box" to oppose any possible Italian advance into Egypt. Roughly 15 kilometres square, the "box" as it was known, consisted of a maze of section posts, weapon pits, dugouts, communication trenches and tank traps, surrounded at strategic points with barbed wire entanglements. Bill Glue wrote at the time: "To us new arrivals it looked like hard work with picks and shovels, and it certainly was – barbed wire and sandbags everywhere. The digging varied from soft sand to rock too hard for our picks and shovels; the pioneer platoon's crowbars were in constant use."

Jack chose a good position for his tent, dug it in and walled it with sandbags. It was a wise choice. A heavy November downpour flooded the dugouts (the "cut and covers" as the Army called them) and all the tents built in low-lying wadis.

One of Jack's jobs was to bring some captured Italian trucks to Baggush. At this stage in North Africa it was expected that the Italians might attempt a drive on Alexandria at any time.

On 5 October 20 Battalion celebrated the anniversary of their entry into Burnham Camp. They had been one year exactly in the army. They celebrated with beer saved for the occasion.

Winter nights in the desert were unbelievably cold. Jack would wrap up in an overcoat, a balaclava, two jerseys, two shirts, a woollen singlet and long trousers, and he was still cold!

Jack looked forward to mail from home. It was always good to arrive back at Base after being away to find a stack of letters waiting for him. Eunie was a prolific writer and was always sending him letters and postcards. Jack had to be careful what he wrote to Eunie, and to his family, as each letter was censored for security reasons.

One of the characters in the 2 NZEF was Lieutenant-Colonel Lindsay Inglis. He was known as "Whisky Bill", probably for obvious reasons. He later became a major-general. He had commanded a machine-gun company in France during World War I, and in the opinion of Howard Kippenberger "was a thorough soldier". In the years after the war Whisky Bill would often stay with Jack when he was working in one of his pubs, and after drinking all night would invariably drive all the way home to Auckland.

In December Italy's General Graziani crossed the frontier with his army, and this move led the men to believe that they would shortly see some action. When nothing happened they became angry and disappointed.

Training continued, and the men learned a great deal about adjusting to life in the desert environment. Then the N.Z. Division was asked to carry supplies for General Wavell's offensive in the Western Desert. They had to establish petrol dumps behind the advancing 7 Armoured Division and then pick up prisoners-of-war and bring them to Mersa Matruh.

On 30 December a convoy of 20 Battalion trucks were shelled when they were sent to pick up infantry of the Australian 2/7 and 2/11 Battalions when they went in to attack Bardia. An Italian radio broadcast caused great hilarity amongst the troops with the report that the Italian soldiers defending Bardia had shown exceptional bravery against "800 tanks and 400,000 men".

The men now had cause to celebrate. The Italians and Libyans were taking a pounding from the Australians in the first Libyan campaign. The Christmas mail and Patriotic Fund parcels had arrived from New Zealand. The New Year of 1941 came in with a roar.

On 11 January the Division prepared to move to Helwan, 30 kilometres or so up river from Maadi. The men were at Helwan for a month, and during that time they completed more training. When reinforcements were added to the division, it added fuel to another rumour from Lord Haw-Haw.

The men were ready. As Kippenberger wrote to a friend in New Zealand: "We have not wasted our time. We are ready. My men will do their whole duty."

Jack spent a period of time at Gezira on internal security, and then in early March 1941 moved with the rest of the 20th to Amiriya, a dusty transit camp in the desert, about 20 kilometres from Alexandria. Jack handed in his kitbag, blankets, palliasse and mosquito net. That night they pooled their food parcels in one glorious fry up.

The night before the men arrived in Amiriya, the Australians marked their disapproval of its facilities by setting fire to the camp cinema! It would seem that these desert cinemas were never to meet with the satisfaction of the troops.

It was at this time – March, 1941 – that the situation in the Balkans prompted Winston Churchill to call for reinforcements. Peter Fraser and the New Zealand Government had grave misgivings on this point, but reluctantly and conditionally agreed to the New Zealand's participation in the Greek campaign. The most important condition was that plans for an evacuation should be drawn up immediately, but this, and several other provisos were never fulfilled.

Lord Haw-Haw announced on the radio that General Freyberg's circus was on the move, and Jack and the rest of 20 Battalion received orders to embark, destination unknown. The men had no idea where they were going. That would come later, when they were at sea. Rumours were rife, and guessing games were on; speculation ranged from the Far East to the Dodecanese Islands.

Jack said goodbye to the Western Desert for the last time. For him there would be no return. At Alexandria Jack boarded HMS *Breconshire*, a naval oil freighter, and spread his groundsheet and a blanket on the steel deck covered with the greasy circles of oil barrels. The convoy was made up of four cargo ships, a troopship, two Royal Navy cruisers, and two destroyers. The *Breconshire* sailed at 5 o'clock on 12 March. Colonel Kippenberger read an order from General Freyberg informing the men that they were on the way to fight in Greece "for the protection of Greek civilisation."

On board the ship in the Aegean Sea the men encountered the worst storm, according to the sailors, that they had experienced in a long time. As they came in view of the island of Crete, with its snow-capped mountains, Jack was reminded of the last time he had seen New Zealand and Mt Egmont.

The men disembarked at Piraeus and they were amazed to see crowds of people lining the streets of Athens. They gave the men a tumultuous welcome throwing flowers and handing them wine. The excited welcome given to the Kiwis by the Greeks was in direct contrast to that given to several hundred Italian prisoners who had marched through the streets of Athens to the accompaniment of derisive boos and hisses.

Jack was excited to be in another country, and loved Greece. His first impressions were of olive trees, white-washed stone houses and orange trees. The Greek landscape reminded him again of New Zealand, particularly the South Island. The hills surrounding the city of Athens extended to rugged snow-capped mountains from which swept icy winds.

At this stage Germany was not at war with Greece, and the German Embassy, with its swastika flags hanging from the balcony and jack-booted storm troopers with swastika armbands standing in the doorway, was still operating in Athens.

Leave was granted to 20 per cent of the battalion at a time and Jack took great delight in visiting Athens. He found the people friendly and willing to show him around the city. He visited the Acropolis and many historical places. He frequented many of the small wineshops which sold a particularly agreeable wine, mavrodaphne.

Whilst on leave Jack could not help noticing the shabby Greek soldiers in the streets, with the toes cut out of their boots to ease the pain of frostbite. These men had been fighting the Italian divisions in the mountains of Albania. Sixteen Greek divisions chased 27 Italian divisions back into Albania and trapped them in the mountains. It was hard not to compare these Greek soldiers with the tall, well-built Evzones in their immaculate short kilts, long white stockings and shoes with pompoms.

Jack, always concerned for the welfare of others, and knowing that the Greeks were desperately short of food, purloined as many supplies as he possibly could and gave them to the starving Greeks, who were grateful to receive butter, cheese or canned meats.

The local children appeared healthy and hungry and seemed to have a craving for sugar which, unfortunately, was hard to come by. Jack and some of the other men played with the children, and taught them to count in English. They, in turn, taught them some rudimentary Greek. Simple greetings, for example, "Good morning, Good evening, How are you". The children also tried to teach the men a catchy tune about Mussolini – "That funny fellow Mussolini", and what the Greeks would do to him when they won the war.

Very soon there was two-way trading between the children and the men. A young boy, Andreas, brought in three dozen eggs to Sergeant Jack Johnson. He tested each one by shaking it near his ear and he finally rejected one egg as being suspect. Andreas laughed and dropped the suspect egg on the hard ground where it broke – it was perfectly good.

The children were not used to motor vehicles and they developed a craze for swinging on the tailboard of the trucks while in motion. The drivers had to take great care when they started up the trucks, and fortunately there were no serious injuries among the children.

The Division assembled for the first time since the war was declared and busily prepared defensive positions on the Olympus Pass. On 18 March they packed up to go to the front. One or two had already found the local firewater, koniac, uzo and retsina, and had to be helped along on the march to the station. They were on their way north to Katerini, a Balkan town 24 hours away by train. Six officers and 80 other ranks, including Jack, were left behind in an infantry reinforcement depot at Hymettus near Athens under the command of Major Archie MacDuff. Jack was put in charge of hundreds of bombs which were stacked in large depots and he had about 20 men to help him. These bombs were to be ready for use at a moment's notice.

He had been there two or three weeks when a major and a colonel arrived at the bomb depot one day. The major was Garth Dutton, an old friend whom he had not seen for a long time. They had played rep football on the West Coast long before the war. Years later, when the war had long finished, Jack met up with him again in Opotiki.

There were few men left in Greece – most of them were away fighting. Scores of women and old men worked in the fields and on the roads.

It was clear that the invasion of Greece was imminent. The Germans were already in Bulgaria, and Jack wondered what was going to happen next. No one, not even the top brass, seemed to know anything, and as Private Jack Spicer of the 20th Intelligence Section remarked: "Never in the field of human conflict has so little been known by so many about so much!"

On 6 April 1941 Germany declared war on Yugoslavia and Greece. The day before the New Zealand Division had become part of 1 Australian Corps with 6 Australian Division and other British troops under General Blamey's command. German tanks and mechanised forces took Salonika, advanced swiftly into the Florina Gap and threatened to drive through the Servia Pass and outflank the New Zealand line of defence. The New Zealand

Division, under Blamey's command, had the task of holding a second line from Mt. Olympus along the Aliakmon River to the west. For Jack and the rest of the 20th, their moment had come at last. Now their real war was to begin.

–6–
CHASED OUT OF GREECE

**"THE MOUNTAINS LOOK ON MARATHON, AND
MARATHON LOOKS ON THE SEA; AND MUSING
THERE AN HOUR ALONE I DREAMED THAT GREECE
MIGHT STILL BE FREE."**

– LORD BYRON –

After the Greek divisions chased the Italians out of Albania,
Hitler, predictably furious with Mussolini's bungling of the situation, sent one of his favourite generals, the brilliant Erwin
Rommel, or "Desert Fox" as he was to become, of the Western
Desert, to sort out the mess and try to save the Italian army. The
Italians were on the run in North Africa where 40,000 British
forces had captured an estimated 130,000 Italian soldiers. Before
the situation could get any worse, Hitler dispatched Rommel and
500,000 German soldiers to take Greece.

Three weeks after arriving to defend Greece against the fast-
moving Germans, Freyberg wrote in his diary: "The situation is
a grave one; we shall be fighting against heavy odds in a plan that
has been ill-conceived, and one that violates every principle of
military strategy."

Some historians liken the Greek campaign to that of Gallipoli
during World War I. That disastrous landing on Turkish soil in
1915 had been a military nightmare, also sanctioned by Winston
Churchill and with a costly loss of life. It has since been recorded
that Churchill wondered at this time whether history might repeat
itself. Perhaps he was thinking of this fact when he wrote: "I did
not, however, give up hope of a final stand at Thermopylae" he
wrote. "The intervening ages fell away. Why not one more
undying feat of arms?"

After the departure of 20 Battalion for Katerini on 18 March,

YUGOSLAVIA
BULGARIA
METAXAS LINE

MONASTIR
MT KAIMAKCHALAN
Florina
Vevi
Amindaio
Edhessa
ALBANIA
Kastoria
VERMION
Ptolemais
Veroia
SALONIKA
Kozani
Stendhami
Kitros
Prosiliono
Gannokhora
Servia
Katerini
SERVIA PASS
Dholikhi
Ay. Dhimitrios
PINDUS RANGE
Dhieskati
Elasson
Rimnion
MT OLYMPUS
Platamon
Kondeleimon
Grevena
Eleftherokhorion
PINIOS GORGE
Dhomohikon
Tempe
Ioanina
Kalabaka
Tirnavos
AEGEAN
Trikkala
Larisa
SEA
Pinios R.
VOLOS
Pharsala
Almiros
N
THERMOPYLAE LINE
Sethis
Lamia
Gapu Knimis
Molos
Longos
EUBOEA ISLAND
Brallos
Livanatais
Klinsokhori
Atalandi
Levadhia
Khalkis
Theber
Patrai
Kriekouki
Marathon
Rafina
Elevsis
PELOPONNESE
Corinth
Daphni
ATHENS
CANAL
PIRAEUS
Porto Rafti
Nemea
Markopoulon
Kea Island
Argos
Miloi
Navplion
IONIAN
SEA
Tripolis
Kalamata
Sparta
Monemvasia

GREECE
Legend
- - - - - - ROADS
+-+-+-+ RAILWAYS
+++++ INTERNATIONAL BOUNDARIES
GROUND OVER 600 METRES
GROUND OVER 1000 METRES

0 5 10 20 30 40 50
SCALE OF MILES

74

its reinforcements moved from Hymettus to the New Zealand Division reinforcement camp at Voula. Small groups of men formed detachments around Athens, Piraeus and the docks. Yugoslavia had suddenly capitulated, the Germans were approaching rapidly from the south, and Greek resistance had collapsed. The Aliakmon line would have to be abandoned and there was no alternative but to retreat.

On 21 April Jack and the rest of 20 Battalion received news that Greece would have to be evacuated, and the next day they received orders to organise reinforcements for a fighting battalion to act as a rearguard when 4 Brigade (the Division's rearguard) came through. However, there was hardly any transport and no equipment, so the men had to do the best they could. They had to help themselves in the Athens stores as there were no guards. They did find some Lewis and Vickers guns and some explosives, but on the whole they were severely short.

After a conference in Athens, Major MacDuff issued orders to move out that night. It was Anzac Day and Jack, together with the rest of the convoy, left Athens at 7.00 in the evening. They passed through Elevsis, Megara, and Corinth, and reached Argos at dawn.

On the same day German parachute troops and gliders landed at Corinth. They seized the bridge over the canal which would cut off all the British troops to the north and prevent the planned evacuation south of the Peloponnese. With the destruction of the bridge the Fourth Brigade were evacuated from Porto Rafti, south-east of Athens.

With the capitulation of Greece people evacuated their villages, leaving behind their hens and pigs, some of whom surrendered to the battalion's cooks. Inside most of the village houses there was a Greek flag, ready to be hung on display for the next victory in Albania. There was now little to celebrate in Greece.

In the meantime the rest of 20 Battalion were also on the retreat. Theirs was a rush against time – the Germans were said to be landing parachute troops in Australian and Greek uniforms. "Shoot first – ask questions later", were the men's orders. The Battalion's real war had begun for them on Good Friday, 11

April. They had been in Lava, a hill village overlooking the Servia Pass. That evening German bombers and fighters roared over and bombed and strafed the pass road to Servia. In Lava the villagers left their cottages as darkness fell and moved into caves in the hills for the night. Old men with antique rifles were left to guard the village.

The following day a German reconnaissance plane flew over attacking Servia, followed by twenty dive-bombers in the late afternoon.

In amongst heavy cold and rain the men of the 20th had no option but to move at short notice to another position at Rimnion, where they once again dug in and tried to snatch a little sleep between air raids. Then they were off again back to Lava, some in trucks, but most of them on foot.

One of the most dangerous places on the pass road to Servia was known as "Hellfire Corner", which seemed to be continually bombed and strafed by enemy planes. The Germans obviously knew that the men were withdrawing and gave the village a real pasting. The men finally reached Larisa where they caught up with an Australian and British convoy heading south. It wasn't easy being on the run from the Germans. Most of the journey had to be done on foot where the men were continually exposed to dive-bombers. Very often they would just pass through a village only to be caught on the road and machine-gunned by a squadron of fighter-bombers. It was a case of every man for himself, finding whatever cover he could. The planes would fly up and down with the guns firing flat out.

Brigadier Jim Burrows in his book *Pathway Among Men* wrote that the New Zealand soldier was "tough, rough and sometimes bad. With other soldiers around him, he hates to be caught out in the act of kindness, and a gruff manner when dealing with the locals is more often than not assumed for the benefit of his mates. But at heart he is the kindest and softest character who ever gave away a shirt. In a city like Cairo, where beer was plentiful and his thirst was great, the Kiwi soldier was too often in trouble, and on pay nights particularly, his image was not good; but in Greece among unprotected women, old men and

76

children, he was magnificent."

As the retreat continued the Royal Navy began to evacuate British and Anzac troops. Six cruisers and 19 destroyers rescued the retreating forces over the next six days. General Freyberg had been under orders to leave earlier, but he refused as his men were still fighting.

German radio jeered at the Allied effort, playing a British song:

"Run rabbit, run rabbit, run, run, run,
Bang, bang, bang, goes the farmer's gun..."

Freyberg realised after the air raid on Corinth on the night of 25/26 April which ended with the seizure of the city by the Germans, that there was no other course but evacuation, and that the best place was the port of Kalamata. The 26th of April was spent on the road by convoys of men, their nerves shattered and near breaking point. One of the worst and most harrowing sounds to the men was the piercing scream of the Stukas as they dived towards them before releasing their bombs. After each attack, when the men would make a dive for the ditches on the side of the road, inevitably they would see trucks and other vehicles in flames after a one-sided battle. The Germans had the skies to themselves.

In the late afternoon of 26 April Jack, together with the rest of the 20th reinforcements, camped in some olive groves several kilometres north of Kalamata. Archie MacDuff conferred with an English officer, Brigadier Parrington, who was responsible for the embarkation plans. MacDuff returned with the news that they were to be ready on the wharf the following morning.

The port of Kalamata was surrounded by bracken-cloaked hills, stunted mountain oak trees, colourful orange and olive groves, and tall cypress trees. It would have been a beautiful place for a holiday in peace-time, thought Jack. Just then it was crammed with thousands of British, 16 and 17 Australian Brigades and Corps troops, Palestinian and Cypriot labourers, Yugoslav soldiers and refugees, Indian mule drivers, Lascar seamen, and New Zealanders, including men from the 28th (Maori) Battalion.

The New Zealanders were caught up in the confusion of the withdrawal – many had lost their units, others had moved south with the hospital casualties after the bombing of the "Hellas" in Piraeus Harbour, while still others had escaped from the Corinth Canal.

During the evening of the 26/27 April approximately 7,000 mainly Australian troops were taken off in destroyers which ferried them to two transports. Prospects for the evacuation of the New Zealanders the following day looked good.

One man from the 4th Field Artillery was Albie Thompson who arrived in the port of Kalamata on the late afternoon of the 27th of April.

"No one seemed to know what was going on – there was much confusion, and there were so many people milling around. That night we lined up on the beach as we had been told that the Navy would be coming in that night. Unfortunately no ships arrived, and we had to go back into the olive groves which were outside the town for the rest of the night."

Around the 28th of April there had been two German forces moving south into the Peloponnese – the 111 Battalion SS 'Adolf Hitler' Division from Patrai and 5 Panzer Division from Corinth. The former went down the west coast to Pirgos, and on 29 April, when the railway line was found to be undamaged, a reinforcement company was sent to Kalamata. This reinforcement company found parts of the 5 Panzer Division, which included two companies of paratroopers already established in the area. Because of this, an advance guard of 5 Panzer Division on the evening of the 28th of April were in time to prevent the embarkation of 7,000 men, of whom many were New Zealanders.

When the Germans arrived at the opposite end of the town they captured the naval liaison officer. There was no organised fighting, only small bouts, sometimes with an officer, and sometimes with a sergeant. Major Archie MacDuff tried to arrange for people to go out in parties to do something constructive. Albie Thompson takes up the story:

"I was with a group who was trying to clear the Germans out of one part of the town, and we were engaged in hand-to-hand fighting, going from street to street. By this time it was dark, and we had to continually dodge tracer bullets, watching them go up the street. I hoped like hell I wouldn't cop it. About this time we came across a 2lb anti-tank gun, and being artillery men, we thought we would get it down to the waterfront to have a go at the big Jerry guns which were giving us a lot of trouble. Unfortunately, one of the chaps who was pushing it around must have bumped the firing mechanism with the disastrous result for an Australian lieutenant who happened to walk in front of the gun just at that particular time – he was killed instantly."

There had been approximately 16,000 men at Kalamata, all of them hoping for embarkation. When on the night of the 27th of April 7,000-8,000 mainly Australians were evacuated, along with

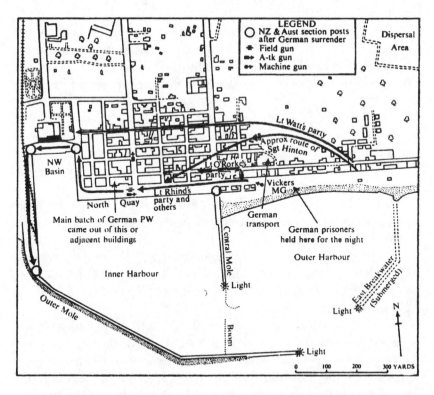

THE BATTLE FOR KALAMATA WATERFRONT, 28-29 APRIL

the crown jewels of Yugoslavia in the destroyer *Defender*, 8,000 men were left behind, mostly from base units. The area commander, Brigadier Parrington, assured senior officers that embarkation was possible the following night.

Jack had arrived with the New Zealand Reinforcement Battalion on the 27th of April on the outskirts of Kalamata, and he noticed that the Germans were using 6 inch mortars. The Reinforcement Battalion drove their vehicles through the town to the assembly area near the junction of the Beach Road and the Link Road.

There he saw columns of men moving hopefully along the Beach Road towards the harbour. They were told later that there would be no embarkation. The next day, 28 April, saw more air raids and more casualties, until by nightfall there were 200 military wounded in the Greek hospital.

A plan by Major MacDuff to cover the approach to the waterfront by "A" Company of the 20th Battalion was never put into action. Already the advance guard of 5 Panzer Division had overwhelmed a group of 4 Hussars. No warning could be given to the New Zealand Reinforcement battalion as much of that unit was already in Kalamata. Several parties of men were taken prisoner, and of those who broke away, some were successful in escaping. Others were shot and wounded. However, the Germans met with little opposition, and capturing still more prisoners, they moved on into the town.

W.G. McClymont states in his official history *To Greece* that the Germans were obviously surprised at the number of soldiers about the town.

"...The important fact was that there was no serious opposition. The majority of the Allied troops were already to the east of the town; the rest were drifting along the tracks and side roads to the assembly areas..."

Although the Germans had no idea exactly how many troops were in Kalamata, when more and more bunches of men were taken prisoner, and put into the already-crammed Custom House building by the harbour, they realised the situation was dangerous. They expected a counter-attack at any minute, and they

80

questioned the prisoners very closely to see how many men were at the other end of the waterfront.

By now of course the several thousand men hiding in the olive groves realised that the Germans were gaining a solid foothold in the town. Once this was known lorry drivers rushed back from the hospital area yelling out that there were Germans in the town. Regular bursts of machine-gun fire were heard, word came that the road through the town was blocked by the enemy, and men could be seen running back to the safety of the olive groves.

Jack was amazed to hear Brigadier Parrington ordering the men to surrender.

"Surrender?" said Jack incredulously.

"Go and jump in the bloody lake!" he said.

"I'll have you court martialled for speaking to me like that!" said Parrington.

"If you're not careful" said Jack, "I'll have you court martialled for talking surrender!"

Jack noticed that Parrington was a World War I soldier. Instead of wearing battle dress, he was dressed in a frocked coat complete with side-arms (his revolver in the holster).

The first serious opposition seems to have come from Major Basil Carey, 3 Royal Tank Regiment. Carey had been walking towards the harbour with Major Pemberton of the Royal Signals when the news that the Germans had gained a foothold in the town reached them. Carey collected a Bren gun and spent the next two hours on the seaward side of the Beach Road, firing at the German guns on the quay and encouraging anyone who wanted to fight.

Lieutenant-Colonel H.H.E. Geddes, Royal Army Service Corps, gathered as many troops as possible and joined Carey, learning something of the German positions. Then he returned to the olive groves and organised parties to clear the streets parallel to the waterfront.

It was about this time that Jack met up with Basil Carey. Carey came from Essex from a well-to-do family and was a real character, according to Jack. He was to get to know him well. He always wore a black patch over an eye he had knocked out

81

opening a bottle of beer before the war.

Carey was in a slit trench when he first met Jack. A good-humoured banter took place between the two of them:

"I'll give you covering fire if you will put that gun out there!" said Carey to Jack. And Jack said to him:

"I'll give you covering fire if you'll put out the bloody gun!"

However, Jack knew that the major was right. Something had to be done and quickly. There were between 5,000 and 6,000 men at Kalamata waiting to be evacuated.

At about 5.43pm that night five German armoured cars entered the town and cut off the quay where a possible embarkation would take place. An account of the situation at this time was written in the 20th unit history:

"At dusk we started to move towards the town, and about half a mile from the outskirts, Major MacDuff met us and distributed grenades and small-arms ammunition. He was shouting to us to get into it and saying that unless the town was cleared, the Navy would be unable to take us off. Nearing the town we encountered fire from a large calibre gun, a heavy mortar, armoured vehicles and machine-guns... An LMG which had given considerable trouble was cleaned out by grenades. I made contact with Jim Hesson, Doug Patterson, and Jack Hinton, all of the 20th..."

While all this was going on another source of resistance, and one of the major ones, was the New Zealand Reinforcement Battalion. Lieutenant O'Rorke and Captain Rhind had been sent to see that the covering companies went into position. On their instruction Captain Simmonds with men from "B" Company, Lieutenant Bricket and his platoon, and Lieutenant Jim Moodie from Headquarters Company moved back to cover the Sparta Road on the eastern exit from the town. They were approached by troops in trucks yelling "Jerries in town!" and by Greeks who called out "Germania!" Moodie knew the latest technique in street fighting and he and his men pulled down stone walls and prepared a defence post. O'Rorke and Rhind returned to the road junction, collected about 20 New Zealanders and Australians, and moved towards the enemy.

As soon as he heard the sound of firing, Jack had gone to the Headquarters corner and tried to find out what was happening. Nobody seemed to know what was going on – there was such confusion everywhere. On the Beach Road leading to the town he collected some New Zealanders, among them Alan Jones and Doug Patterson. They all agreed that the big gun on the waterfront which opened up on the men, must be put out quickly. However the machine-gun fire all round them was so heavy they had to turn south up a side street, and then go forward again a block or two inland from the waterfront.

It was now dark in the street and Jack could just make out the small white-washed houses. In his hand was a .303 rifle with fixed bayonet and in the pocket of his shorts were several hand grenades. These were ready to be used at a moment's notice. At any moment he expected a German to fire at him from the cover of a doorway. His heart started to beat fast, and he tried to calm himself. This was his one chance, he thought, to make some form of resistance.

It was hard to see what was happening, except for the sudden clarity after a flare went up. All around him mortar bombs were exploding and tracer bullets were being fired up and down the street. Suddenly he heard firing close by and he glimpsed the field-grey of German uniforms. He saw a machine-gun post at the corner of the street, and with one deft throw he wiped it out with one of his grenades. The eastern and northern approaches to the street were now covered. All around him Jack could see dead Germans lying about. He was strangely impersonal about them. The medics will take care of the wounded he thought. He had to move on.

Together with Jim Hesson, Doug Patterson and Alan Jones, he took over control of the German LMG, and conferred on the next plan of action. They huddled together, out of sight of the enemy. All the time the fire from the German mortars was coming closer, closer to the men. They could hear the sound of the heavy gun firing on the beach, together with the LMGs which were giving covering fire to the heavy weapons.

"How are we going to put those bloody guns out?" said Jack to the other men. "We've got no decent bloody weapons, and there's only a few of us against all of them."

In the middle of their discussions, without any warning, a large fat German stepped out from behind a house and let fly with a Spandau. Jim Hesson cried out with pain as a bullet ripped into the flesh of his arm, severely wounding him.

"I'm going to get that effing bastard!" shouted Patterson in a fury. Jack grabbed his arm and said: "Hang on! He's probably long gone. We'll clean out the Jerry position first. We'll get him, don't worry."

"To hell with this! Who will come with me?" yelled Jack, and then to Alan Jones, "Give me covering fire!"

He then proceeded to work his way along the street, using doorways for cover as far as possible.

Afterwards, Jones was to write in the 20th unit history: "I consider any man who was prepared to accept my covering fire should have been awarded the V.C. for that act alone!"

Jones tried to use the German LMG as there was plenty of ammunition for it. "Christ! Wouldn't you bloody know it!" he swore. "This bloody thing is stuffed! We'll have to use the Bren!" They were in the middle of the street with German machine-guns firing at them from the windows of several houses.

Jones stood up and fired with the Bren. While he was doing this a German on the balcony was shooting at him with a captured Tommy gun. Bullets were hitting the post. Afterwards they found that flakes of concrete chipped off the post had cut the German around the throat and eyes.

The two men started running in the direction of the big guns on the waterfront with Jones keeping a line of fire just out from the buildings on the same side of the street. Jack wondered if Jones and the others were feeling the same as him. He felt pent-up; he could feel his heart pounding in his chest. This is it now, he thought. I've got a job to do and I have to do it. He was scared, shit-scared really, but over-riding these feelings, he had a sense of crazy excitement, almost as if there was some invisible force egging him on, and he was caught up in it. It was telling him to do these mad things, throw his life to the wind. Suddenly, he knew without a doubt why he had travelled all these thousands of kilometres. Everything he had done in the last year was in preparation for this moment. It was so clear to him he almost laughed out loud. In the back of his mind he could hear Eunie calling him, telling him not to be a fool; he could see the gentle face of his mother, and with those two images in his mind he set off. He would get through, somehow.

Jack ran as fast as he could down the street towards the waterfront. He knew there were Germans hidden inside some of the houses. He could see them firing from the windows. With one swift movement he smashed open the door of a house with his boot. He threw some grenades inside, and then continued on to the next.

"Jonah!" Jack shouted to Jones, who was just behind him. "We'll just take this last house, and then have a go at the guns. I haven't much ammo left!"

About fifty yards from the guns Jack came across two men in a doorway. He was on the point of bayoneting them, thinking they were German when one of them yelled out in English. He recognised one of them as the medical officer, Major "Two-Pill" Thomson. Thomson at that stage was endeavouring to find MacDuff to inform him of the location of the nearest RAP (Regimental Aid Post), as he was mindful of the fact that the New Zealanders might shoot first and ask questions later, or throw grenades.

Jack ran to within several metres of the nearest gun. The gun fired, just missing him. It was now or never. With every ounce of strength in his weary body, he hurled two grenades one after the other, at the gun. He had no time to think, evaluate his actions. He could hear the cries of the wounded, smell the gunpowder and smoke in the warm Greek night. He put his hand in his pocket and drew another grenade. It was his last. Almost at the same time a truck loaded with Australian and New Zealand troops turned on to the waterfront and pulled up sharply with a squeal of brakes to within 50 metres of the first gun. The crew dashed for cover up the nearest side street and opened fire on the German crew about the gun.

As Jack threw his last grenade at the gun a German rushed out from behind a building. The German lifted his Spandau and fired point-blank at him. Jack just had time to see a flash of field-grey before he felt a blow to his stomach. He looked down and saw his boots filling with blood, his blood. How odd, he thought. He must have been hit. He felt dazed, and suddenly he was hit by waves of nausea, which enveloped him like a sheet As he tried to fight down feelings of panic the world around him started to spin, spin into ugly black grotesque shapes; his legs buckled underneath him as he lost consciousness and fell to the dusty ground.

–7–
ONE CROWDED HOUR

"THE PATH OF DUTY WAS THE WAY TO GLORY."
– TENNYSON –

The fighting on the waterfront of Kalamata continued, spontaneous and irresistible, from one building to another. Major "Two-Pill" Thomson, the New Zealand doctor, was captured by the Germans. They gradually withdrew, taking their prisoners with them, and leaving the Regimental Aid Post, or RAP as it was known, which had been set up by Thomson, to the British.

In the confusion and chaos of the battle Albie Thompson, trying to keep his nose out of trouble, suddenly saw a New Zealander dash out of a side street to take the second large gun on the waterfront with hand grenades.

"I found out it was the forcefully-spoken Jack Hinton and that he had been wounded in the stomach."

After Jack was shot, Alan Jones, who had met up again with Doug Patterson, carried on the fight. Jones was caught up with the excitement, and Patterson wrote later in the 20th Battalion and Armoured Regiment's unit history that Jones had told him that "it was the best night he had had since he left New Zealand." In one street five German armoured vehicles were parked. The crews were upstairs in one of the houses and seemed to be firing from the upper storeys. Jones and Patterson fired at them and at the ones who made a dash for their vehicles. The noise from the machine-guns was deafening and the air was thick with fumes and dust. The men could hardly see as it was pitch dark. Now the remaining Germans left in the house were firing from the bottom windows, and Jones stood up and fired with the Bren. Bullets were hitting the post of the house and Patterson was just thinking what a rotten shot Jonah was when he saw it was a German on the balcony firing at him. Jones relentlessly kept firing at the light machine-guns until he was hit in the shoulder and fell across Patterson's feet. Patterson immediately took control of the Bren, swinging it in the direction of the German on the balcony. As if in slow motion, the German stumbled and, clutching his stomach, fell backwards over the balcony on to the footpath below. Suddenly all went quiet. The Germans in the house had stopped firing.

When the firing stopped Patterson ran across the road and threw some grenades through one of the open windows. A few minutes later a crowd of Germans came out through a door in a corner of the building with their hands up. At the same time a small group of Kiwis came around the corner from an adjacent street. They immediately confronted the Germans with Patterson. One of the Germans, speaking almost perfect English, said:

"You'd better look after us because our main party will be here in an hour."

Patterson took the wounded Alan Jones to the RAP. Some Australians were there and they gave the two men some brandy. Although he was in pain, Jones wanted to continue the fight and asked for a captured Mauser as he could no longer carry his Bren.

An officer told Patterson that he and the others should go up the Corinth Road, turn any trucks sideways to block the road, and set them alight.

"We parked the trucks across the highway" said Patterson, "but I don't remember anyone setting them alight."

The men then returned to Kalamata. After Hinton, Jones and the other men of the advance parties were wounded, reserves hastened forward from the olive groves. There seemed to be no shortage of men to continue the fight. By midnight the Germans had surrendered to whoever was near – the final number was over 120 all ranks. Their casualties had been heavy, particularly about the more forward of the two heavy guns. In all there were 41 killed and over 60 wounded. The British casualties were three officers and 30 other ranks killed and 50 or more wounded.

New Zealander Lieutenant Pat Rhind led his own small party which gallantly engaged in hand-to-hand fighting in the streets of

Kalamata. One member of his party could speak German and he called on the Germans to surrender. In a few minutes the Germans, about 80 or 90 of them, gave themselves up. The prisoners were sent back to the beach under escort and an attempt was made to tip the heavy gun into the sea, but it jammed against a tree. They turned a truck around to face out to sea, and with the headlamps, signalled to the Navy that the waterfront had been cleared, and that they were ready to embark. Unfortunately there was no reply. They organised parties to carry the wounded to the RAP.

When they were told that Brigadier Parrington was going to surrender they decided to make a break for it, but before they got far they were rounded up by a German motor-cycle patrol.

"The Germans retreated from the town leaving us in control" says Albie Thompson. "They didn't realise there were so many of us there. We could see the Navy out at sea, but we didn't know any code words to tell them to come in, as the Naval Liaison Officer had been captured. I was talking to some of the Tommy signallers and they told me that one of their chaps had made contact with a chap on board a cruiser from his home town. He found out they had been to the same school and knew the same teachers. The Navy took that to be authentic and sent in a destroyer."

The cruisers *Perth*, *Phoebe*, destroyers *Nubian*, *Defender*, *Hereward*, *Decoy*, *Hasty* and *Hero* approached the harbour. Unfortunately there was a shortage of boats and there was little time to get off the sick and wounded. In the end only 332 all ranks were evacuated.

"The Tommies flashed a signal saying: 'Sorry, the Italian Navy is coming. Goodbye, best of luck'" said Albie Thompson.

On that night of 28 April the first stages of surrender were prepared by the British. Brigadier Parrington based his decision to surrender on the fact that it would save needless loss of life. There were several reasons why he felt surrender was the only course of action. He described the situation in his diary as at 1.00am on 29 April. He said his force had had undisputed possession of the quay since 11.00pm. German prisoners had stated that they were the advance guard of a panzer division which had landed at Patrai. The British forces had no rations left and nearly all of its ammunition had been used up. The vast majority of the 10,000 troops in Kalamata were without arms. There were 250 wounded and no medical supplies. As well as all this, most of their transport was destroyed.

"Intensive enemy air action would commence at daybreak" wrote Parrington, "and no action of ours could prevent the enemy from placing his heavy artillery where they could bring fire to bear on the port...which would effectively prevent any further attempts at embarkation. In these circumstances it seemed to me that no useful military purpose could be served by offering further resistance.... I proposed to inform the enemy that no further resistance would be offered after 0530 hours; that...any officer or man was free to make his own escape if he could, and that present positions would be maintained until 0530 hours to allow this to be done."

In the early hours of 29 April the men heard German tanks and infantry cars and trucks in the hills, and they were told that the Senior British Officer, Brigadier Parrington, with an interpreter, had made contact with the Germans to surrender. Captain Kennard of 4 Hussars was sent back with a German officer to say that the force would surrender before daybreak. At 6.00am the Allied forces at Kalamata officially surrendered to the Germans. The men lined up on the beach and watched as some Germans arrived in a large staff car bearing a swastika. They laid swastikas around the troops in case the Royal Air Force should bomb the beach after the surrender.

It was about this time that Dr Thomson, who had earlier been captured after surrendering to an enemy advance party, and who had remained with the wounded near Kalamata, rejoined the men and told them that even though they were prisoners they were still soldiers.

"We marched out of this big area into a field on the other side of the town," said Albie Thompson. "Two-Pill told us to march like men, and we did, with our heads up, even though we were now prisoners of the Germans. I think the Jerries respected us, because at that stage in the war they were good front-line troops."

"I saw a Maori sergeant who was leading his men with a bayonet as we had no ammunition left, and he led them down a side street towards a German machine-gun. He must have had his mouth open very wide as he yelled at them, because he took a bullet right through one cheek and out the other."

For the Allied troops at Kalamata it was all over in a few hours. The tragedy of Kalamata was that there was little direction, little ammunition and medical supplies, many of the troops were unarmed, and by the time it was decided to cease fire in the early hours of 29 April, there was little darkness left for anyone to escape to the hills through the surrounding German posts. A few men managed successful escapes, but the majority were rounded up in the first few days. Also, when the warships finally did arrive to take the men off, only a few hundred could be taken on board.

The 20th Battalion and Armoured Regiment's unit history refers to the fighting at Kalamata as gallant and heroic.

"Whatever the final result may have been," it says, "20 Battalion is proud of those who fought at Kalamata, and glad that the defiant heroism of Jack Hinton, fittingly rewarded with a Victoria Cross, the reckless courage of men like Alan Jones, and the fighting spirit of quiet chaps like Doug Patterson, Pat Rhind, Jim Hesson and Bob O'Rorke so ably upheld its honour in the field."

"...the fight at Kalamata, when little groups of New Zealanders and Australians armed only with rifles and bayonets, grenades, a few machine guns and the pathetic Boyes anti-tank rifles, recaptured the town from the advanced guard of a German Panzer Division equipped with machine guns, mortars, and two field guns, ranks as an infantry action of the highest order."

The Germans claimed Kalamata as a victory. A German "Propagandakompanie" produced an account of the action at

Kalamata for home consumption and extracts from it give a reader today some idea of how the Allied resistance bubble swelled up before it finally burst:

"We had torn through the Peleponnesus at the double.... Everywhere on the road southward the attacking unit of a panzer division, thrusting with lightning speed, was receiving the surrender of little groups of stranded Tommies.... In Kalamata too it appeared that the Britishers meant to surrender.... But in the course of the afternoon things changed.... Things were so quiet. Then rifle fire began to crackle in the harbour; isolated shots at first but then it suddenly swelled to a hurricane.

And now the mass of Britishers comes on to attack....They come out of the side-streets, jump from house to house, shoot from the windows and threaten to overwhelm the handful of Germans by sheer weight of numbers.... The fire-power of the company can no longer hold the British out.... Now the Britishers are simply welling up out of every garden and lane. There is hissing and spitting. Ricochets moan over the heads of the German marksmen.... The Company commander collects what men he still has....

"Only 2 MGs are still firing. Hand grenades explode. The Britishers try to break in. They get within three metres.... We cannot shoot until the enemy can be plainly seen in the darkness.... Like cats the Australians jump from walls and windows on to the German marksmen.

"Now it is 10 p.m. The house to house struggle has become in part a wild hand to hand sruggle...Then towards 11 p.m. one of the wounded Britishers shouts with his last strength: "Fire stopping!" He shouts it after a German bullet has brought him down at point-blank range."

Jack reached up to the edge of consciousness and gripped it with the tip of his fingers. He was afraid if he didn't do this he would fall down into that bottomless black void again. Even that slight movement of his fingers caused every part of him to cry out in agony. He gradually became aware of shapes hovering around him, and as his vision slowly began to clear, his mind told him that if he lay very still the pain might go away. Someone was holding a bowl in front of him. He must have been sick in it many times, he thought. Slowly he became aware of his surroundings. He seemed to be lying on a makeshift bed on the ground in some olive groves. He was aware that he was strapped down; his chest felt heavy. He opened his eyes fully now. The sky above him was a vivid blue. It reminded him of a long time ago when he was lying on the beach at Colac Bay on a hot summer's day. He could feel the heat of the sun beating down on him. So I'm alive, he thought. Someone was speaking to him soothingly, and he recognised the doctor, "Two-Pill" Thomson. In the same instant another, more urgent thought registered in his mind. He needed to go to the toilet. In a hospital it would be no problem, but here, in these olive groves?

"Give me a bottle," he muttered weakly to Thomson. "I can't move."

"Don't try and move" said Thomson. "I'll get you something."

In a minute he was back carrying a dark red claret bottle without a label.

"You'll feel better once you've used it" said Thomson. "Be very careful. You have a nasty wound and you are still bleeding heavily. I'll help you."

Jack felt that even that simple act had taken him to the edge of a precipice and back again. He kept perfectly still. He realised he was still in shock. His mouth felt dry, as dry and parched as if he had not had a drink for several days.

"How long have I been here?" he asked Thomson.

"For several hours. We've surrendered all our weapons and more Germans have come in on troop carriers. We're waiting now to get you to a makeshift hospital where you can be properly treated," said Thomson.

For the rest of that day and part of the next, Jack was looked after by Thomson and an English doctor, a Dr Grey. There were many other wounded men in the olive groves, and it was almost a relief when the Germans came, put the wounded on stretchers,

93

and took them to an old house in Kalamata. There Jack's wounds were properly treated. The bullet from the Spandau had pierced his bladder and rectum and damaged his stomach. He was unable to eat and was continually thirsty. All around him he could hear men groaning and being sick. Most were calling out weakly for water.

W. Wynne Mason writes in his unit history *Prisoners-of-War* that the Germans treated their prisoners courteously and fairly, and that their medical officers assisted Allied medics in emergency dressing stations for the 250 British wounded. In particular at Kalamata the Germans treated their prisoners-of-war humanely, and serious cases like Jack's were evacuated as soon as possible to Greek hospitals where allied medical officers were given facilities to treat them.

After a couple of days Jack and the rest of the seriously wounded were taken by truck to a hospital in Kokkinia near Athens. The hospital building had been a polytechnic school, and was a large white-stoned building high on the hillside between Piraeus and Athens. It was surrounded by barbed wire and German guards. Hospital arrangements and surgery were run by an Australian doctor, Major Brooke Moore, who was aided by a staff of Australian and British doctors with male medical orderlies. The makeshift hospital was large enough for 500 wounded, but with more and more wounded arriving each day from the battle of Crete, it soon had to cope with over 700. A walking-wounded and convalescent camp was established in some old Turkish barracks just below the hospital on the outskirts of Kokkinia.

Wounded men were lying in the passages of the hospital and beds were crowded together in the wards with little space between them. There was a great shortage of food, despite help from the Greek and Red Cross funds, which, especially in dysentery cases, inhibited patients' recovery.

Under these difficult circumstances Major Brooke Moore and his staff did a wonderful job, and many prisoners owe their lives to the splendid work carried out by these doctors. Many of the medical staff had volunteered to stay behind to look after the wounded when Greece was being evacuated and heavy casualties were expected from the beaches.

Sid Bishop of the 2/5th Australian General Hospital was part of a group of volunteers who stayed behind in Greece to look after the wounded after they had field treatment. The hospital was under canvas except for administration, at Ekali.

"In many cases the wounded had sparse treatment – in some cases no treatment at all." says Bishop. "The situation was grim. The only place one could be sure of getting treatment was the morgue! At the hospital in Kokkinia where I later worked there was a grave shortage of essential supplies. I don't know how we managed. There were three floors at Kokkinia and we had trouble getting the wounded up the stairs."

Jack had just arrived at the hospital when 400 Germans walked in and one said to him: "Fur Sie der Krieg ist vorbei." ("For you the war is over!")

Jack just grinned at him and said, "Yes, I would like a cigarette!" He was amazed when a short time later the German returned with a packet of 20 Players cigarettes!

In New Zealand and in Egypt very little was known about the desperate action at Kalamata. In letters home New Zealanders in hospitals in Greece and Germany wrote of Hinton's courage and leadership. Some also wrote to the Red Cross in London.

Meanwhile, Jack, lying in a crammed ward in the hospital, had no idea that he would be the recipient of the most coveted medal for bravery six months hence. His condition was still serious, and he was in a great deal of pain. He was given opiates for it, and for some time it was such a relief to give in and allow a wave of relaxation and peace to envelop him like a shroud. The pain would vanish, and his mind would become peaceful and calm.

Jack found life in the ward monotonous and dull after all he was used to. As his wounds started to heal and his pain subsided, he wondered how he would ever get used to life as a prisoner-of-war. He had no idea how long the war would go on, and the thought of years stretching ahead interminably filled him with despair. Depression was a common ailment in that hospital in Kokkinia. Not only were the men ill and badly wounded, but their diet was inadequate, which meant most of them did not have the stamina to fight despair. Breakfast consisted of a half slice of Greek brown wholemeal bread and a mug of ersatz coffee. The bread was dry or had some sour type of jam on it. The coffee was made from roasted acorns ground up. There was no milk or sugar with the coffee. Lunch consisted of a plate of hot "soup" – thin water with a few beans floating in it and sometimes a trace of horse meat. With it there would be another half-slice of bread. Occasionally there would be some coarse rice pudding to feed them up. The evening meal was another half slice of bread and a mug of coffee. It was a starvation diet and within a few weeks Jack had lost more than 12 kilograms.

Had it not been for the Greek Red Cross Jack could not have survived those early months in Athens. Through the parcels the men's diet was supplemented once a week with fruit and other foodstuffs. This was mainly through the efforts of the head of the Red Cross, Madame Zannas and her helpers, who were tireless in their efforts to procure food and comforts for the men. Doctors in the hospital told the men that they owed their lives to their efforts. Occasionally Madame Zannas and her helpers were allowed to go into the wards and speak to the men, always accompanied by German guards.

Inevitably, conversation amongst the men would always turn to the subject of food. They would concoct delicious meals until they were silenced by protests from some who could not bear to listen any longer.

The men became ingenious at passing the time. Those who were well enough, played cards and attended bridge schools. Others did arts and crafts, created various objects out of pieces of wood or read books, which were at a premium. Even the oldest of books were read with the greatest pleasure.

As Jack gradually became stronger, and as soon as he was able to get out of bed, he tried to take a small walk each day. At first just the effort of putting his feet on the ground made him giddy and lightheaded, but by the end of the first week he was able to slowly walk the length of the ward. In the following weeks he increased his exercise, until finally, about three months after his capture, he was able to reach the top roof of the hospital. This was where all the men went, once they were able to walk, as the roof was bathed in sun. The roof was up a flight of 20 steps or more, and Jack found the climb exhausting. However, once he reached the top he found the view breathtaking. The sun shone down on him, warming every part of him. Far below him stretched the city of Athens, the white-stone houses and buildings glowing with the heat of a summer's day. In the background Jack could see the hills which swept around to the coast, and Piraeus Harbour cluttered with small boats and ships. To the east the turquoise Aegean Sea sparkled, and just below him stood the ageless beauty of the Acropolis. The scent of wild herbs hung in the air. Jack stood very still drinking in the exquisite beauty of the scene. He felt too overcome to speak. He thought of Eunie, his mother and his family back home in New Zealand, and what they would be doing. By now they would know that he was safe, although wounded, and that he was a prisoner-of-war. In that moment he was determined that somehow he was going to survive, whatever the future held.

News of Jack took time to reach his family back home. In May they were told that he was missing, and it wasn't until mid October that they knew the nature of his injuries and where he was:

NEW ZEALAND POST OFFICE TELEGRAPHS
OFFICERS, N.C.O.'S AND MEN REPORTED, MISSING

TO: MRS H G HINTON
     COLAC BAY
     SOUTHLAND

MUCH REGRET TO INFORM YOU THAT YOUR SON 7930
SGT J D HINTON HAS BEEN REPORTED MISSING THE
PRIME MINISTER DESIRES ME TO CONVEY TO YOU ON
BEHALF OF THE GOVERNMENT HIS SYMPATHY WITH
YOU IN YOUR ANXIETY.

                          F. JONES
                          MINISTER OF DEFENCE

                          25th June, 1941.

Mrs. H.G. Hinton,
Colac Bay,
SOUTHLAND.

Dear Mrs. Hinton,

    On the 26th May the Hon. the Minister of Defence informed
you by telegram that your son 7930 Sergeant John Daniel Hinton
was missing. Advice has now been received to the effect that he
has also been reported wounded, and it would appear that he was
wounded prior to being posted as missing.

    This is the only information which has so far come to hand,
but confirmation or otherwise of all such reports is expected in
the near future, when I will again get in touch with you and, I
hope, relieve your anxiety.

                        Yours faithfully,
                        R.S WOGAN
                        Director

NEW ZEALAND POST OFFICE TELEGRAPHS
<u>OFFICERS, N.C.O.'S AND MEN PREVIOUSLY REPORTED</u>
<u>MISSING NOW PRISONER OF WAR</u>

TO: MRS H.G. HINTON
     COLAC BAY
     SOUTHLAND

FURTHER CABLE REPORTS THAT YOUR SON 7930 SER-
GEANT JOHN DANIEL HINTON PREVIOUSLY REPORTED
MISSING, HAS NOW BEEN REPORTED PRISONER OF WAR
IN HOSPITAL GREECE THE PRIME MINISTER DESIRES ME
TO CONVEY TO YOU ON BEHALF OF THE GOVERN-
MENT HIS SINCERE REGRET.

                    F. JONES
                    MINISTER OF DEFENCE.

                        13th. October, 1941.

Mrs. H.G. Hinton,
Colac Bay,
SOUTHLAND.

Dear Mrs. Hinton,

    Cabled advice has just come to hand from overseas giving
some further information concerning your son, Sergeant John
Daniel Hinton, who was reported to be a prisoner of war in
hospital. It is now stated that he is in hospital at Kokinia in
Greece, and that he is suffering from Gunshot Wound in Abdomen.

    In conveying this news to you, I wish to express my sincere
sympathy, together with the hope that the soldier is receiving all
attention possible, and that he will effect an early recovery.

                    Yours faithfully,
                      R S W
                    Director

At about the same time as this news of his whereabouts was given to his family, Jack was sent for by a German guard. He was told to report immediately to the Orderly Room, and wondered if he was going to be accused of some crime. His heart beat fast as he walked through the door. To his amazement he saw the whole German guard lined up outside the office, and feared the worst. Then, a corporal stepped forward and the whole guard saluted him. With great ceremony he was ushered into the office where he was told that he had won the Victoria Cross. News had come through to the hospital from Geneva of the award, and Major Brooke Moore had spoken to the Germans and they had put on a guard-of-honour.

Jack felt as if he was dreaming; he had to pinch himself to make sure he was still alive. In his own words he thought that there must have been some mistake – that "it was a lot of bull". Brooke Moore then came into the office and laughed heartily at Jack's amazement and confusion. He found it ironic that a man should be congratulated by his enemies for killing them. But Brooke Moore had told the Nazi commander that the Victoria Cross was the highest award for bravery that the King could bestow. Even the Nazis upheld the virtues of courage and gallantry and held them in high esteem. The Germans offered Jack the freedom of the city, but he refused because he was too ill.

FROM: The High Commissioner, London
TO: The Prime Minister, Wellington
DATED: 15th October, 1941
DATE AND TIME OF RECEIPT: 16th October,1941 5.25 p.m.

SECRET   IMMEDIATE

M.L.1884. His Most Gracious Majesty the King has been graciously pleased to approve of the award of the Victoria Cross to 7930 Sergeant John Daniel HINTON, 20th Battalion, New Zealand Military Forces. To permit of simultaneous announcement being made in New Zealand and British Press this award will be announced in the London Gazette Friday, 17th October, 1941 and in the Press on the following day. Following is copy of citation which will appear in the London Gazette Begins:

King has been graciously pleased to approve of the award of the Victoria Cross to the undermentioned:-

7930 Sergeant John Daniel Hinton, New Zealand Military Forces On the night of 28th April, 1941 during fighting in Greece column of German armoured forces entered Kalamai. This column which contained several armoured cars 2 inch guns and 3 inch mortars and two 6 inch guns rapidly converged on large forces of British and New Zealand troops awaiting embarkation on the beach. When order to retreat to cover was given Sergeant Hinton shouted, "To hell with this, who will come with me?" ran to within several yards of the nearest gun the guns fired missing him and he hurled two grenades which completely wiped out crews. He then came on with bayonet followed by a crowd of New Zealanders. German troops abandoned first 6 inch gun and retreated into two houses. Sergeant Hinton smashed windows and then the door of the first house and dealt with the garrison with bayonet. He repeated the performance in the second house and as result until overwhelming forces arrived New Zealanders held the guns. Sergeant Hinton then fell with a bullet wound through the lower abdomen and was taken prisoner. Ends.

Please send preferably through Reuter immediately on release all possible homely details about Hinton for Press here especially about his civil occupation parents whether prominent in sport also photographs by Clipper mail. Press upset no such details sent from New Zealand of Upham and Hulme. Repeated Fernleaf.

(Signed)   JORDAN

OUTWARD

FROM   :   C.G.S. ARMY H.Q. WELLINGTON.
TO   :   N.Z. LIAISON OFFICER C/o. HIGH
                     COMMISSIONER LONDON
DATED   :   20th OCTOBER 1941

A4899.
PLEASE CONVEY TO 7930 SERGEANT JOHN DANIEL
HINTON 2ND NEW ZEALAND EXPEDITIONARY FORCE
REPORTED WOUNDED PRISONER OF WAR KOKINIA
HOSPITAL GREECE FOLLOWING MESSAGE FROM MINIS-
TER OF DEFENCE BEGINS.
IT GIVES ME VERY GREAT PLEASURE TO INFORM YOU
THAT HIS MAJESTY THE KING HAS BEEN GRACIOUSLY
PLEASED TO APPROVE OF THE AWARD OF THE VICTO-
RIA CROSS TO YOU FOR OUTSTANDING GALLANTRY
AND LEADERSHIP IN GREECE. THE PRIME MINISTER
DESIRES ME ON BEHALF OF THE GOVERNMENT TO
CONVEY TO YOU HIS WARMEST CONGRATULATION ON
THIS GREAT HONOUR CONFERRED ON YOU AND TO
EXPRESS THE HOPE THAT YOU WILL SOON BE RESTORED
TO HEALTH. YOUR MOTHER HAS BEEN ADVISED. ENDS.
ALSO FOLLOWING MESSAGE FROM MAJOR-GENERAL
PUTTICK CHIEF OF THE GENERAL STAFF BEGINS.
MY HEARTY CONGRATULATIONS ON AWARD OF VICTO-
RIA CROSS AND BEST WISHES FOR SPEEDY RECOVERY.
ENDS.

Wing Commander Edward Howell, later to win the DFC and the
OBE, was a patient in the hospital at Kokkinia. He became a firm
friend of Jack's and later wrote a book on his wartime experi-
ences. He mentions the incident of Jack being congratulated on
winning the V.C.

"...One day they brought us news that a New Zealand sergeant, who was a patient in the hospital, had been awarded the Victoria Cross. The news had come through Geneva. The whole hospital rejoiced with him in this high honour, and he came round to our ward so that we could congratulate him. His name was Sergeant Hinton."

The news of Jack's award travelled around the world, and the *Christchurch Press* published a long account of an interview with Major George Thomson, who had recommended Jack for the V.C.

"...Describing Sergeant Hinton's courageous stand against all odds as the small Allied party was trapped, Thomson said: 'I could see some of our soldiers not far away from the truck I was travelling in. There was quite a lot of noise and movement. Firing broke out as the German party drew near and I heard a British officer's voice shouting: 'Take cover, men, take cover!' I heard another voice yelling: 'To hell with all this take cover! Who's coming with me?'

"...The Huns ran into several houses. Sergeant Hinton burst in the door of the first house, throwing hand grenades and then led his men inside with their bayonets. A shambles must have followed his entry because when he came out his bayonet was literally dripping blood.

"With his men behind him, he raced across to the next house. Some men fell, but Sergeant Hinton and the remainder cleaned up the second house, and it was when he was still pursuing the Germans running down the road that he was shot in the abdomen."

Thomson jumped from the truck and started across to Hinton, but was fired on by the British party, who later explained that they thought Thomson was a German in British uniform. Thomson had Hinton lifted on to a truck and taken to hospital.

Thomson told the NZEF Official News Service that every man killed or who died at Kalamata was buried correctly with honours in a small plot of land at the back of the town.

Besides the great care given to the Kiwis by Dr Thomson at Kalamata, two other men gave courage, cheerfulness and great spiritual comfort. These were the Reverend R.J. Griffiths and the Reverend R.J. Hiddlestone of Auckland who volunteered to stay with "his boys".

On Saturday, October 18, 1941 it was publicly announced that His Majesty the King had approved the award of the Victoria Cross to Sergeant John Daniel Hinton of the Twentieth Battalion of the New Zealand Military Forces. The citation was published in the *London Gazette*.

"On the night of April 28th-29th 1941 during the fighting in Greece, a column of German armoured forces entered Kalamai. This column, which contained several armoured cars with 2-inch guns and 3-inch mortars and two 6-inch guns rapidly converged on large forces of British and New Zealand troops awaiting embarkation on the beach. When the order to retreat to cover was given, Sergeant Hinton shouted "To Hell with this! Who will come with me?"

He ran to within several yards of the nearest guns. The guns fired but missed him and he hurled two grenades which completely wiped out the crews. He then came on with the bayonet, followed by a crowd of New Zealanders. The German troops abandoned the first 6-inch gun and retreated into two houses. Sergeant Hinton smashed the windows and then the door of the first house and dealt with the garrison with his bayonet. He repeated the performance in the second house and, as a result, until overwhelming German forces arrived, the New Zealanders held the guns. Sergeant Hinton then fell with a bullet through the lower abdomen and was taken prisoner."

The citation was also published in every newspaper in New Zealand, and the *Southland Times* published this special post-script at the foot of the citation.

"Even in captivity, and suffering from a painful wound, you showed that bravery is not just a thing of action on the battlefield, for yours was the spirit which preserved cheerfulness and faith in yourself and your companions through days of dreary discomfort and galling loss of liberty."

-8-
SALONIKA – CAMP 183

"OFTEN THE TEST OF COURAGE IS NOT TO DIE BUT TO LIVE."
– ALFIERI –

As soon as Jack was well enough to leave the hospital he was put in the walking-wounded camp at Kokkinia. Conditions at the camp, nicknamed the "Con" camp were dreadful. The "Con" camp was a former Turkish army barracks. The majority of the prisoners were infested with lice and there was no sanitation. It was a real hell-hole, according to Jack, and because there was a chronic shortage of food, the prisoners started to suffer from blackouts. This was common in prisoner-of war camps where food was very short.

There were no beds in the "Con" camp – only concrete floors to sleep on, and no blankets or bedding of any description, unless anyone was fortunate enough to have brought some with them. Drinking water came from primitive wells. The men also had to use the wells for washing and this water was restricted. Each man was allowed about 300ml of water a day.

There were huge, open trenches for latrines built by the Turks years earlier. These unsanitary conditions attracted hundreds of flies, and in the heat dysentery spread like wildfire. One English soldier was so incensed with the whole situation that he dropped a lighted match into the latrines and blew them up!

As far as diet was concerned in the camp, Jack lived mainly on a thin watery soup with a few lentils floating in it. Because of his stomach wounds he was unable to eat the army biscuits which were also available as well as black bread and potatoes. Once again the Greek Red Cross came to the men's aid supplying occasional meat as a much-needed supplement. Soon Jack was suffering from malnutrition.

While Jack was a prisoner in Kokkinia he was pleased to meet up with three familiar faces – George Brown, minus a leg, Jack Bain, who had been wounded, and Bill Nisbet, also wounded.

The Greek people were quite unafraid to show their sympathy and friendship to the prisoners in full view of the German guards. Jack remembers one or two Greek men in Salonika spitting on the ground with contempt in front of two German guards – there was no secret of the hatred they felt for the invaders of their beloved country.

As the war progressed conditions in Greece became so critical that men, women and children were starving. But in 1941 and 1942, at the time when Jack was a prisoner, although food was far from plentiful, the Greeks managed somehow or other to help the prisoners with gifts of fruit, cigarettes or any other item of food, especially bread, which at that stage in the war was virtually unobtainable.

Jack gradually adjusted to life in the "Con" camp – it took a lot to upset him, but he determined to escape if he possibly could. One day at a camp athletic meeting he sat with several other POWs as two New Zealanders practised pole-vaulting. To his immense surprise and delight he saw the two New Zealanders vault over the obstacle perimeter wire, which was about 1.8m in height, land safely on the other side and head for cover in the thick bush nearby. The guards were so amazed that for a moment or two they just stared at the retreating figures before they raised their rifles and shouted in fury. These two courageous men were Donald Stott and Bob Morton who later became secret agents for Special Operations Executive. Their escape from the infamous "Con" camp was one of the first daylight escapes made from a POW camp.

Late in November, 1941 news was received that the prisoners were to be transferred to a camp at Salonika en route for Germany. One morning soon after, Jack was one of a group of men herded together with whatever possessions they had, loaded into buses and taken down to the harbour. There they were entrained on the Italian hospital ship *Gradisca*. The *Gradisca* could carry between 200 and 300 wounded. Half the crew were German and the rest were Greeks, who made it quite clear to the prisoners that the despicable Germans were their temporary masters only.

It was a five-day voyage to Salonika, and for the first time since Jack had been captured at the end of April, he received good food. On board the ship were Italian medical officers and sisters who provided excellent nursing care to the prisoners, most of whom, like Jack, were still recovering from wounds. As well as decent food Jack's sleeping quarters were good with comfortable bunks.

Once again Jack was embarking on a sea voyage, and as he had done before, he stood on the deck with some of the other men as the *Gradisca* steamed out of Piraeus Harbour. He had grown to love Greece and its people and even though he was a prisoner-of-war and his freedom had been taken from him, he felt something akin to sadness to be leaving Greek soil. Again he wondered what the future would hold for him. He wondered how long he would be in Salonika – it could be weeks or months before he was sent on to Germany.

On board the ship that evening Jack was served a wonderful meal. He could hardly believe it when he saw white bread, meat and potatoes on his plate, and he could even buy a bottle of beer from the German canteen. He thought it almost too good to be true but he slept very well that night.

The journey continued across the Aegean in brilliant sunshine until the ship entered the Gulf of Salonika. Mt Olympus stood massive and stark to port, its snow-capped peaks superb and magnificent. A patrol of Messerschmitts flew over in complete formation, dark against the sky, the sun glinting on the tips of their wings. They circled the ship and then flew back to the mainland.

Jack watched the planes. He would accept whatever happened now, he thought. He felt that his life had already been mapped out for him, and that nothing he did would alter that, however much he fought against it. It was almost as if he had lived through all this in another place, another time. It was the same sort of feeling that he had had when he had run through the streets of Kalamata, when he did not know if he would survive or be killed. Jack usually kept his feelings to himself, but on the voyage to Salonika he conveyed something of what he was feeling to one or two of the men he had become close mates with.

When the ship arrived in Salonika it tied up at the quay and then the men were herded over to where trucks were waiting to ferry them to their new camp. Each truck was guarded by a soldier with a machine-gun. If anyone had any thoughts of making a break for freedom this was quickly dismissed from his mind.

The trucks took off with a loud squeal of tyres from the quay disturbing a flock of gulls who rose screeching in the air as their peace was disturbed. They rumbled along the cobbled streets, each man absorbed in his own thoughts. How long would they be in Salonika, how long would they be prisoners? What would the camps be like in Germany, and would they ever see their homes again?

Almost all prisoners-of-war captured in Greece and Crete who did not escape passed through the transit camp at Salonika known as Frontstalag 183. Some men stayed only 24 hours; others were kept there for up to several months to do forced labour for the Germans.

Jack lined up with the other prisoners at the entrance to Camp 183. A German Feldwebel screamed at them, "Any man attempting to escape will be shot!"

The camp was an old disused Greek barracks on the outskirts of the town, and it had an infamous reputation. If Jack thought that the "Con" camp at Kokkinia was the pits, 183 was doubly so. The buildings were in a state of ruin, thick with filth and infested with lice and fleas. It was impossible to sleep because of the bedbugs, and a plague of rats which had the run of the complex. As with the "Con" camp there were no blankets or other bedding, and the men had to sleep on rough concrete floors. At the end of each barrack was only one water tap and four filthy latrines to cope with hundreds of prisoners.

Because many of the windows were missing a bitterly cold

draught blew constantly into the buildings. Each barrack room had one small stove around which the men huddled for warmth but a chronic shortage of fuel meant every stick of furniture, which included various doors in the compound, was used for firewood.

The food was worse than what Jack had experienced in the "Con" camp. It consisted mainly of a watery soup with the occasional vegetable floating in it, and some mouldy bread. Apart from a drink of water, which was rationed, there were two hot cups of German 'mint tea'. Diseases like beriberi and malaria were common, as Salonika was in the centre of a malaria belt. Yet again, the Greek Red Cross came to the aid of the prisoners, whenever it was able. It provided milk, brown bread, rice, fruit, vegetables and eggs, and cigarettes for the hospital patients when available.

W. Wynne Mason writes that the lack of conditions were the direct result of a lack of provision and supervision by the German High Command, whose main attention had been directed elsewhere.

"...Apparently the German line-of-communication authorities on the spot imposed little if any check on the acts of brutally-minded guards, and delayed granting permission for delegates of the International Red Cross Committee or of some other neutral power to inspect the camp."

At opposite ends of the square were wooden towers. Sentries stood in these towers with loaded machine-guns. At night searchlights swung from one end of the camp to the other. It looked as if escape would be impossible. Stories of how men had been shot trying to escape circled the camp; their bodies had been left hanging on the wire until morning. However, the camp was riddled with tunnels in various stages of completion. One or two of these had been discovered and had been blocked up.

The routine of the camp was similar to that of the "Con" camp. "Appell" or roll call, was twice a day. All able-bodied men had to go outside for this and form up in two ranks. The sick and badly wounded had to sit by their beds or in the wards while the Germans went around to check their names off on their lists. Each morning the Kommandant would inspect the camp. Jack would stand by his bed, together with the rest of the prisoners, as the Kommandant came around. He was always accompanied by two British warrant officers who spoke good German.

It was at Salonika that Jack met up again with Basil Carey. He too, had been captured at Kalamata and soon the two men had become firm friends. Carey had never had to fend for himself and he had no idea how to cook or to boil water. Each man had been issued with a billy which they used to boil water. Carey had to ask Jack what to do with the billy and if he could show him how to boil water! Soon the weather became very cold with the temperature plummeting to below zero. Snow lay deep on the frozen ground. As December progressed the cold became almost unbearable. Jack froze without a greatcoat. He had been given some clothes from some British prisoners, but they were mainly shorts, shirts and underclothes. As there was little fuel he and some of his friends decided to cut down the lavatory doors for firewood. Of course when the Germans found out there was hell to pay.

Exercise was the only way of keeping warm. Jack would pace up and down the perimeter wire, his hands deep in the pockets of his jacket.

In the meantime back home in New Zealand in Colac Bay, tributes had been pouring in to the Hinton home. Jack's parents had been leading a quiet life in retirement as all their family had left the district. Now suddenly, their lives changed. The following telegram was delivered to them on 18 October.

NEW ZEALAND POST OFFICE TELEGRAPHS.

TO: MRS H G HINTON
     COLAC BAY
     SOUTHLAND

IT GIVES ME VERY GREAT PLEASURE TO INFORM YOU THAT HIS MAJESTY THE KING HAS BEEN GRACIOUSLY PLEASED TO APPROVE OF THE AWARD OF THE VICTO-

RIA CROSS TO YOUR SON 7930 SGT JOHN DANIEL HINTON FOR OUTSTANDING GALLANTRY AND LEADERSHIP IN GREECE(stop) THE PRIME MINISTER DESIRES ME ON BEHALF OF THE GOVERNMENT TO CONVEY TO YOU HIS WARMEST CONGRATULATIONS ON THIS GREAT HONOUR CONFERRED ON YOUR SON AND TO EXPRESS HIS SINCERE HOPE THAT YOUR SON WILL SOON BE RESTORED TO YOU SAFE AND SOUND

F. JONES
MINISTER OF DEFENCE

From the first moment when the telegram had been delivered in person by the Postmistress, Miss Ogren, feelings of incredulity had been followed by fierce pride; that their son had achieved the highest honour of all – it was so unexpected. The *Southland Times* reported that:

> "...Visitors, including total strangers, have stepped over the spotless doorstep for a kindly handshake with the parents of the man who has brought honour to his family, his district and his country."

Mr and Mrs Hinton were invited to Invercargill to talk on the radio, Station 4YZ. She told the people of New Zealand how very surprised and proud she had been to hear that her son had won the VC.

> "Although we are very happy about the wonderful news" she said, "it would have been a much happier occasion for us if John had been coming home himself, instead of getting the V.C. We wish to thank all the people from all over New Zealand for the kind telegraph messages they have sent. Knowing John as I do I feel quite sure that he would have been happy if he could have shared this distinction with the rest of the 20 Battalion."

And in 20 Battalion which was by this time back in the Western Desert after the disasters of Greece and Crete, a notice appeared in the unit lines: "Join the 20th and get a V.C."

Lieutenant-Colonel Burrows, who had left the battalion in September to command the Southern Infantry Training Depot at Maadi Camp, sent his unit's congratulations when he heard that the V.C. had been awarded not only to Charles Upham, but also to Jack Hinton. The following letter was sent to Colonel Kippenberger:

Headquarters,
Southern Inf. Trg. Depot
18 Oct 1941

MEMORANDUM FOR:
H.Q., 20 Bn,
2nd NZEF.

HONOURS AND AWARDS

Reference our communication 11:1:4630 dated 15 Oct 1941, for '2nd Lieut Upham' read '2nd Lieut Upham and Sergeant J.D. Hinton.'

It would be a convenience to this headquarters if in future the names of members of the Twentieth Battalion who win Victoria Crosses were published in one list and not on different days as appears to be the present practice.

(Sgd) J.T. Burrows
Lieut-Colonel

Years later, that same letter was published in an anthology on military subjects *The War on Land* by Brigadier W.F.K. Thompson, who wrote that he got "particular pleasure from the memorandum on Honours and Awards, signed by Lt-Col. J.T. Burrows, 20 Bn 2 NZEF."

The 20th Battalion had certainly established a splendid record for itself in a short time. Besides the award of the Victoria Cross to Jack, 2nd Lieutenant Charles Upham had also been awarded the Victoria Cross for superb gallantry during the battle for Crete. Others from the 20th who had won awards were Warrant Officer V.D. Kirk, who won the D.C.M., Lieutenant-Colonel Howard Kippenberger, who won the D.S.O. in Crete, and Captain C. Wilson who was posthumously awarded the Greek Military Cross.

On the West Coast Eunie, fiercely proud of Jack, received a letter from one of Jack's closest mates, Sergeant-Major Harvey Grooby from C Company, 20 Battalion.

"Well Eunice" wrote Grooby, "I reckon you are feeling very proud of your little John Daniel, but you can't be any more so than I am of him. I can tell you that I didn't half stick my chest out as I had always predicted that he'd win one. We are all also very pleased with the company's record too, as we have now no less than two V.C.'s 1 DCM, and 1 Greek Cross to our company's credit. Added to that our own battalion commander has the DSO, so you can see that this battalion and company of ours are something to be proud of."

Harvey Grooby, who owned a hardware store in Greymouth, was killed in action in the desert, 1 December, 1941.

Accolades poured in for Jack through various newspapers:

"...a very kind chap, a good joker in every way – an efficient, well-liked NCO very popular with the whole battalion" was the comment of a sergeant who was once associated with Sergeant Hinton in the battalion in Egypt. "I'm not at all surprised at what he did. Nobody who knew would be."

"...Sergeant Hinton's quiet, unassuming manner and generally likeable nature is quoted on all sides by those who have been in contact with him. He is the direct antithesis of the blustering type of NCO, speaking quietly, instructing clearly, and commanding with confidence. On the sports side he is referred to as playing some of the most dashing rugby in matches by the New Zealanders in Egypt. The games were played on makeshift grounds in desert camps. He was also a member of the first of his company's cricket teams...."

Jack also received a letter from the Otago committee of the N.Z. Red Cross offering their congratulations on "the greatest of all honours which has been conferred on you by His Majesty King George VI.... We have a photograph of you in our office of which we are very proud. May we express the wish that you will soon be restored to complete health, that this awful war will soon be over, and that it will not be long before you are back home again in Southland."

In Salonika those prisoners who were able-bodied were put into working parties. This did not apply to Jack as NCOs and officers were not required to work. Also Jack was still suffering from his stomach wounds. Some prisoners in the working parties would use the opportunity of being outside the prison to try and escape. Some of these escapes were successful, but other prisoners were recaptured after a short time on the run. Two escape parties got out through a camp sewer. One man cut his way through a barrack back door, and, dodging the camp searchlights, crawled through the wire and scaled a wall into the street.

It was a strange Christmas for Jack – his first behind barbed wire. Christmas Day dawned fine and cold with a fresh fall of snow. In the long barrack room the prisoners huddled around the stove, the atmosphere cosy and cheerful despite their plight. A service was conducted later that morning by one of the British officers, and the men sang some hymns, one of which "Silent Night", was sung with such feeling by over 200 men. To their amazement some of the German guards joined in the chorus singing "Stille nacht".

Thousands of kilometres away from home the prisoners' thoughts must have been on their families and loved ones, the loss of their precious freedom, the fact that they were hungry, cold, dirty and lousy, with little hope for the future. Many of them were sick, yet they were reconciled with the enemy for a brief time in the true spirit of Christmas.

The men had saved up their rations for this day, and they were rewarded with a Christmas dinner – of sorts. The main dish was roast meat, probably horse, with a roast potato for each man, a Christmas pudding concocted from Red Cross parcels, and red Greek wine. The food helped to lift their spirits as they ate, drank, sang and slept.

The New Year dawned – 1942 – and with it the prospect of another long year in camp. Early in the New Year Jack was told that he was about to be moved to a prison camp in Germany. This news was not unwelcome, because by now he reasoned that any camp in Germany would be welcome after the hell-hole in Salonika. His friend, Wing Commander Edward Howell, was not going with him, but two months after Jack had left the camp, Howell made an amazing escape, getting through to the British lines in Syria.

The people of Salonika turned out en masse to farewell the prisoners as they left Camp 183. They waved to the men and the men waved back. Everybody was smiling and crying at the same time. The men started to sing "Pack Up Your Troubles" and "It's a Long Way to Tipperary". The guards didn't join in the singing. Their faces were sullen, and they marched alongside the men silently.

On arrival at the train the guards shouted at the men: "Schnell! Schnell! On the train! Quick!" Each man was counted by two guards, and they were herded on board like cattle, the green-coated guards prodding the men with rifle-butts, shouting at them, loading and re-loading their rifles. The move from Salónika to Germany was in closed cattle-wagons, and the journey would last from five to ten days, their only rations a few biscuits and half a loaf of bread.

Inside the truck Jack squeezed as close as possible to one of the windows. There were four narrow oblong holes high up on each corner at the side walls. Wooden shutters on heavy iron hinges hung down outside. There were 50 or more men to a wagon and less than half a square metre per person. Whenever the train stopped on its journey, especially at Belgrade, the Red Cross pressed hot soup, food and cigarettes into the hands of the starving men. Lack of water and a complete lack of sanitation were the most serious hardships. Many of the men were suffering from dysentery and kidney disorders. On some occasions the wagons were not opened for 22 hours or more.

The train passed through Bulgaria, Hungary and Austria – their destination Bad Sulza in Thuringia, East Germany. As the train went further north over the mountain ranges approaching Germany, the temperature became colder. Jack sat on the hard floor of the cattle truck. He knew the train was nearing Germany. He caught a glimpse of the passing countryside. He was hungry and desperately in need of sleep.

Suddenly the train came to an abrupt halt. Roughly, the German guards opened the doors of the wagons. Jack jumped down. Burly German guards dressed snugly in greatcoats and sturdy boots with Alsatian dogs on leads stood by the train. Their uniforms were sparkling clean and their boots were polished. Around the station lay mounds of snow, piled high, already turning to slush. It was freezing cold, and a wave of despair hit Jack, as forcefully as if he had been hit by a sledgehammer. He had arrived in Germany.

−9−
GERMANY

"OH GOD – GRANT YOUR STRENGTH TO YOUR SERVANT."
– PSALM 86:16 –

Stalag IXC in Bad Sulza, East Germany, was large and crowded. It consisted of 60 barracks set out in long rows with streets between each row on a huge area of flat sandy land. As well as New Zealanders there were Australian, French, Belgian and Serbian prisoners. Royal Air Force personnel were placed in a separate barrack, and they were not allowed to have their own compound.

Each barrack where the prisoners were locked at night held three-tier wooden bunks, and there were approximately 180 men to each barrack. As well there was additional space for tables and forms. Between the barracks was a small concrete ablutions room and a similar one for washing clothes. The men showered in a separate building.

When Jack arrived in Bad Sulza he received a cup of mint tea and some watery vegetable soup. Two tins of paste and two loaves of bread were also given to the new arrivals, to be divided between nine men.

"Achtung! Achtung! All new arrivals will be deloused. Leave your clothes at the entrance of the ablutions block."

Together with the rest of the new prisoners Jack was herded roughly towards a small building. This was where all prisoners were deloused on entry into the camp. They removed all their clothes which were put into a large boiler and heated for five minutes or so. While the clothes were being fumigated the men went into the showers. It was the first shower for Jack for about six months. It made an enormous psychological difference to him and he immediately began to feel better. When he came out of the shower his clothes were handed back to him. Once a week each prisoner was deloused. Sometimes their clothes were put into ovens, killing the bugs with heat. It was a great relief for the men but unfortunately after a couple of days they would be infested again. Another method of delousing was a fine mist spray, similar to DDT, through which the men had to walk.

In all the time Jack had been a prisoner-of-war he had not received any mail from New Zealand, although he had sent letters home. However, on arrival at Bad Sulza he received a letter from Mr William Jordan, New Zealand High Commissioner to London. The letter congratulated Jack on winning the Victoria Cross. Jack replied immediately, saying he had had a long stay in Greece.

"I am just about my old self again," wrote Jack. He added that he was thrilled on receiving Mr Jordan's letter which was the first since he was taken prisoner.

In Colac Bay his mother was pleased to hear that he had at last received a letter from a New Zealander, for although she had written regularly to Jack his letters indicated that he had not received any mail from her. The last letter she had received from him was dated 14 October 1941. Shortly after, she was officially advised by the authorities that he had been transferred to a prison camp in Germany. She had sent some parcels to Jack and the Scottish branch of the Red Cross had sent her a post card to let her know that he had received them. In his last letter to his mother Jack had told her that he was recovering slowly from his abdominal wounds and he was now able to eat more ordinary food. In reality, his mother would have been horrified if she had known what Jack's diet had been like since he had been captured. All prisoners' letters home were heavily censored, and also Jack had not wished to worry his mother.

At Bad Sulza the food ration for a prisoner was one or two potatoes a day, swede soup with the swede still in it, and a fifth of a loaf of bread made from potato flour with a bit of sawdust. Occasionally there was some horse flesh in the soup. The only medical supply was from the Red Cross. An ordinary Red Cross parcel allowed a second meal a day with a biscuit and a bit of bully beef. It was common for most of the men to pool their parcels. Each morning one of the 180-odd men to each barrack drew the mint tea to the shout of "Mint tea up!"

As soon as a prisoner entered a POW camp he was registered and given a number according to where he was situated. Jack's number was 39448. He was finger-printed and photographed after supplying his name, rank and serial number. Then he was issued with a POW dog tag. Registration as a prisoner-of-war at a camp imparted a new confidence to the men who knew something about the Geneva Convention. All a prisoner's papers and all particulars were sent to Switzerland, and this made a prisoner more secure as the Germans had to account for anything that happened to him. However, many thousands of prisoners passed through German camps without ever seeing a copy of the Geneva Convention, despite Article 84 which laid down that a complete text be put up wherever possible in the native language of POWs "in places where it may be consulted by all prisoners."

One English officer who complained to a camp Kommandant about ill treatment to one of his officers was told that "they (the Germans) had no intention of keeping to the Geneva Convention, which was drawn up by a lot of old women and not by soldiers."

Also Hitler, who was completely indifferent to the welfare of POWs, stated during an after-dinner monologue in September, 1941: "I make no secret of the fact that in my eyes the life of a single German is worth more than the lives of twenty Britishers." After threatening to make British prisoners live with the Russians, he added: "This would make an excellent measure, to which their only counter would be to make sure our prisoners live with the Italians!"

Jack had been in Bad Sulza only a short time when he met Joe Simpson. Joe was a fellow New Zealander who always had a smile on his face, even in the midst of great adversity. He had an enormous sense of humour, and was always fun to be with. He was thick-set, of medium height and a ruddy complexion. He had one thought only, and that was escape. He had already escaped four times from working camps, always to be recaptured. He was never daunted by his failure to escape – he thought it was all great fun. Jack and Joe became great mates, and very soon Joe was aiding Jack in an audacious plan to escape.

On most fine afternoons the prisoners took part in some sporting activity in the compound, watched as always by the camp guards. Joe Simpson was a great sportsman, an old boy of New Plymouth Boys High School where he had excelled in rugby, cricket and swimming. On this particular afternoon he put on a great display of athletic excellence to the shouts and enthusiastic support of the other prisoners. The guards did not seem to notice that the noise seemed to be louder than usual that day. However, it was the fact that they felt compelled to watch as Joe performed some Herculean feats in the high jump.

The guards were so engrossed with Joe's performance that they didn't see Jack edge towards a rubbish wagon standing in one corner of the compound. He quickly climbed into it and one or two of the men covered him with straw from their pillows. Jack had to remain in the wagon until the end of the day, when the wagon, by now piled high with rubbish, was driven to the gates of the camp. There it was stopped by the guards. In the middle of the wagon, Jack, covered with vegetable peelings, cans, bottles, tins and every conceivable type of rubbish, lay perfectly still, his heart beating fast, as the guards poked and prodded with their bayonets around the wagon. By some miracle they did not touch the middle where he was lying. The wagon went slowly through the gates and along the country road leading to the nearest town, and Jack was able to breathe again.

The minutes ticked away, a quarter of an hour, a half hour – how much further until it stopped, Jack wondered. It must have been an hour later, when the wagon came to an abrupt halt. Jack could hear voices and noises around him. He must be in the town, he thought. It was now or never; he had to make a break for it quickly. In one swift movement he threw off the rubbish which covered him, and jumped over the edge of the wagon. He didn't dare look back; he just ran as fast as he could. Behind him he could hear guttural voices shouting in German, and dogs barking. He knew he must get a head start as a German patrol would shortly be on the way. He ran down the narrow cobbled streets, only dimly aware of the amazed stares of people going about their everyday business. He nearly fell over a young boy who ran in front of him to collect a ball thrown in his path.

In his weakened state he found it hard going. His heart was pounding in his chest, and his forehead was covered in sweat. He came to the edge of the town and saw two country lanes in front of him, one leading to the left and the other to the right. He took the left and shortly saw a high hedge looming up in front of him. If he could just get over that hedge.

In front of the hedge was a stile and as Jack was coming up towards it he heard the motor of a car, probably a Kubel van, a short distance away. They're on to me, he thought. With every ounce of strength he possessed, he stumbled over the stile, and threw himself down on the ground, his breath coming in great gasps, and the noise of his heart pounding in his head. Don't let them see me, he prayed. The noise of the van came nearer and nearer, the voices louder and louder. Through a gap in the hedge he could see the grey-uniformed figures, rifles over their shoulders, sitting in the van. Suddenly the van was gone, travelling past him at speed.

Jack ran to the crossroads leading out of town, and took the road to the right. He slowed down to a fast walk, keeping as far as possible to the shady side of the road. It was beginning to get dark, and with the cover of darkness he should have a fighting chance, he reasoned. He kept on walking, one kilometre, two, his legs, unaccustomed to the exercise, becoming tired. His eyes started to close, he fought to keep them open. He was thirsty, maybe he would find a stream, or should he risk asking for a drink at a farmhouse? He stumbled on, and suddenly, before he could stop himself, and just before he came to the end of a country lane, he saw in front of him a patrol of German soldiers with fierce-looking Alsatian dogs on leads.

He stopped abruptly and made to run back along the road from where he had come, but it was too late.

"Halt! Englisher! Halt, or you vill be shot!" There was nothing for it but to stop. Jack turned around to face his pursuers, his hands up in the air. The Germans ran up to him, butting him in the stomach with their rifles. He was roughly handcuffed and viciously propelled towards a waiting truck.

Some time later the truck drove through the gates of Bad Sulza camp to the cheers and boos from the prisoners as they saw Jack sitting between two guards. When the truck stopped Jack was unceremoniously taken to the arrest keller. His punishment, 21 days solitary confinement. His diet, bread and water. Occasionally, there would be a potato, or kartoffel, as the Germans call it, and one slice of black (schwartz) bread.

Part way through his stint in solitary, he was marched out of his cell and into the middle of the parade ground. In front of him stood a German general and three flunkies. Jack was clad in a dirty well-worn short-sleeved shirt, short pants, and wooden boards strapped to his feet to replace the boots he had lost during his capture in Greece. The German general was visibly taken aback by his appearance, as was the camp kommandant. All the spare clothes were in the control of the British officers who were loath to share them with the colonials.

The German general stepped back, took a ribbon from a box, which was a replica of the V.C., and then pinned it on to Jack's shirt. The ribbon had been sent to the camp via the Turkish Red Cross. Then the German saluted and shook hands with him. The Kommandant, through an interpreter, then asked Jack to return to the officers' club for some champagne to toast his medal. After nearly two weeks in solitary, and half-starved, Jack wasn't feeling very kindly towards his jailers, so he told the Kommandant in no uncertain terms to put the champagne up his waistcoat! Years later he regretted his decision – if he had accepted the champagne, he may have spent less time in solitary.

The rest of the prisoners had watched the ceremony, and after Jack had been presented with the ribbon, he was hoisted on to the shoulders of some of the men and carried around the camp.

In a letter to the Red Cross a friend of Jack's revealed that he had received his ribbon at a special parade at the camp.

"We had a surprise parade here last night" he wrote. "There were many wild guesses about the reason when we heard that the German Commanding Officer was attending. He read the official notice that His Majesty the King had awarded Hinton the V.C. I need not attempt to describe how the New Zealander was carried around the camp."

After the ceremony Jack was sent back to solitary again.

While Jack had been in solitary at Bad Sulza, one of his mates from the camp, Thomas Findlay, a dour Scot from New Zealand's 4th Field Ambulance had escaped from a working party near Leipzig. After being put in a civilian jail for a couple of days, he was sent back to Bad Sulza on the same day that Jack was released from solitary. Findlay was sentenced to three weeks solitary in the cell that Jack had just vacated.

Findlay remembers Jack in prisoner-of-war camp, and seeing him being presented with his V.C. ribbon.

"Jack was a very popular man in camp" says Findlay today. "Winning the V.C. never went to his head, and he never changed his personality – he was always friendly and down-to-earth."

Soon after Jack completed his solitary confinement, the camp at Bad Sulza closed down. The Air Force personnel went to a new camp and Jack and the other army personnel were taken to the railway station where they boarded a train for their new camp at Molsdorf.

By now other countries had entered the war. The United States of America had declared war on Japan after Pearl Harbour in Hawaii was bombed. In January 1942 Japan had invaded the Philippines, Malaya and Borneo. Later in the month Burma was invaded and on the 3rd of February Japanese planes bombed Port Moresby in New Guinea. Finally, with the fall of Singapore, and with all of south-east Asia conquered by the Japanese, 26 countries pledged themselves to employ their "full resources, military or economic against the three Axis powers."

There were now many stalags for prisoners-of-war in Germany, East Prussia, Poland and Austria. Official Red Cross sources identified at least 17 camps in 1943 and 34 the following year, although this was nowhere near the actual number of Allied camps.

The camp at Molsdorf consisted of a large group of huts

surrounded by barbed wire which was overlooked by a machine-gun tower equipped with searchlights. Guards patrolled the perimeter with police dogs, while other guards intermingled on the inside. It was dusty and dirty in summer and muddy in winter.

There were Canadians at Molsdorf and many were shackled, supposedly in retaliation for an ill-fated Allied commando raid on the French port of Dieppe in August 1942. The Germans claimed that German prisoners were found shot dead with their hands tied behind their backs.

Apart from the Canadians at Molsdorf, the prisoners were all British, most of them having been captured at Dunkirk with the 51st Division. Corporals, sergeants and sergeant-majors, most of whom had been imprisoned for two years, were treated as privates who were compelled to work while they waited for official recognition.

At Molsdorf Jack met up with Dennis Gallagher. Dennis had been a welterweight boxer in the British army, and he and Jack chummed up. Gallagher had been captured during the battle for Crete. He was shorter than Jack, but tough and stocky in build. He was a marvellous musician and played the saxophone and kept the men entertained for hours.

The Kommandant of Molsdorf was nicknamed "Fish Guts" by Jack because of his big stomach. Before Jack had arrived in Molsdorf there had been a big escape – 86 men had got out through a tunnel. However, they had been recaptured a few days later, and the old Kommandant had been replaced by Fish Guts. Fish Guts was well-liked by the prisoners, and even gave Jack and his friends a radio one day. However, some of the guards took a perverse pleasure in being as unpleasant as possible. When the situation became unbearable Jack or one of his friends would go to the Kommandant and say "Kaput!" The next morning the guard's bag would be packed and he would not be seen again.

Although Jack adjusted to camp life, his main thought was to escape. But, as he learned before, it was not easy escaping from a German prisoner-of-war camp. He decided this time to bide his time and tell only one or two of his closest friends of his plans. Some of his friends had tried to escape from work camps, but as

Jack was a sergeant he did not leave the camp to work. Time for him passed very slowly. It was important for his mental and physical health to keep busy and occupied and he needed a lot of mental stimulation. Many of the men couldn't be bothered, and became what was commonly called "spine-bashers", lying on their beds all day, doing nothing. Some of the men who had musical talent, like Dennis Gallagher, wrote music, while others learned scripts and acted parts in plays. However, the persistent hunger drained a man's strength.

Each man reacted differently to being a prisoner. The only common feeling seems to have been an element of surprise that he should be "in the bag" at all. As one man put it: "I often thought I might be killed or wounded, but it never occurred to me that I might be taken prisoner." However, once a man became a prisoner-of-war there wasn't much he could do about it. Sometimes a prisoner's mind would snap and he would rush at the barbed wire. The guards would shoot him of course, warning fellow prisoners that if they went to help they would be shot also. There was nothing for them but to stick it out.

In the camp at Molsdorf there was a brass band and a recreation hut for entertainment and concerts. Female parts in various productions had to be played by the men. One night the men put on a ballet. The tinsmiths in the camp had managed to make brassieres out of empty tins, and black skirts were made out of black crepe paper. During the performance the men sweated and of course the dye ran everywhere. Jack remembers one man, Benny Elliot, who had a loose set of tin cups. When he did a turn he got so excited that he clapped the tin cups together. It brought the house down.

The prisoners could not have done without the Red Cross. By 1942 relief supplies for POWs had stabilised. In the United Kingdom the British Red Cross had recognised from the earliest days the need for food parcels, and accordingly extra quantities were despatched to Geneva for distribution to POW camps. New Zealand had contributed to a pool of relief food for prisoners from the end of 1941. These food parcels contained mainly cheese, milk, honey and meat, and they were sent overseas at the rate of 6,000 a week.

Special parcels of games were also sent to the camps by the Red Cross, and most camps had been supplied with 14 instruments to make up an orchestra. In addition to hundreds of mouth-organs, ukeleles, and other single instruments, a set of bag-pipes was sent out to the camp. They were played by a Scotsman from the 51st Division who had been captured at Dunkirk. Gramophones and records, sets of sports equipment, team clothing, flower and vegetable seeds were also sent. The Educational Books Section in Oxford also sent many books for study courses at the camp, and by the end of 1942 over 3,500 had been sent to Germany. The men were now able to occupy their time to better advantage with study, and in some cases, to qualify academically for whatever career they intended to pursue in the post-war period.

Jack experienced many night bombing raids while in Molsdorf. One particular winter's night in 1942 he was lying on his bed reading a book when he heard a sound resembling thunder in the distance. As he listened, the noise became louder and louder. He went outside the hut with Joe Simpson where they saw a fleet of Lancaster bombers approaching from the west. There seemed to be hundreds of them – the formation looked about 30 kilometres long and cruising at about 6,500 feet. They were joined by other prisoners as the air raid sirens went off around the camp. Suddenly a hail of high explosive shells from heavy flak rushed up to the approaching bombers. Quickly the men were herded down to the cellars with the Kommandant, the guards and even the dogs during the raid.

Down in the cellar Jack heard the thud, thud, thud of the falling bombs as they burst and cascaded over the city, leaving behind volcanoes of black smoke rising upwards into the brightly-lit sky. Bombs exploded one after the other with slow red flashes. The last of the bombers roared over, leaving behind a scene of death and destruction.

One humorous incident Jack remembers in Molsdorf was when the Canadians were put in handcuffs. They were hand-cuffed during the day, and at night when they had them removed, they also had to remove their boots and trousers, until the next morning. Before long, somebody had fashioned a key to open the handcuffs out of a sardine tin. The guards were amazed the next day when a prisoner took all the handcuffs to the guardroom and put them on the desk. They were never used again!

Another incident that Jack remembers well was when, through an interpreter, the Kommandant was told that the dampness of the camp was very bad for the men's health. Could the prisoners dig a ditch around the camp to drain the moisture? This was allowed and some of the men also started to dig an escape tunnel! While digging the drain the men were escorted by some guards and Alsatians. When the drain had been completed, work was started on the tunnel which was now free of water. The fill from the tunnel was deposited under the prison cells. It took many weeks to dig, and plans were simultaneously made for the men's escape. Those who had done all the digging had first preference. Eventually 52 men escaped from Molsdorf one night in March, 1943. Only one man reached freedom in Switzerland. The rest were recaptured in a few days, and there was hell to pay when they were sent back to camp. The men had been discovered missing when all the prisoners were lined up for a head count. When it was discovered that some were missing the guards and dogs were called in, and photographs were taken of the men left in the camp. Shortly after, the tunnel was discovered and soon filled in.

The time had come for Jack to plan another escape. He and Dennis Gallagher made plans. Escape from Molsdorf was going to be far from easy. An electrified trip-wire sat in front of the 5 metre high barbed wire fence which surrounded the camp. Just beyond that was nearly 2 metres of barbed wire entanglements with a 1 metre overhang which dropped just outside the camp. It would be touch and go if they could bring it off.

One dark night they decided to make the break. It was 9 o'clock and pitch black outside. They had about 90 seconds in which to step over the electric trip-wire and scale the high fence before the camp searchlights would throw their beam on to the fence. The two men crept as quietly as possible and stopped just in front of the trip-wire. There was the beam from the searchlight. They would have to be quick, just over a minute to scale that

128

(Above left) Mary Hinton, 1944.
(Above right) Eunie 1944.
(Right) Jack at Greymouth Railway
Station en route to Burnham Camp,
1939.

Outside Buckingham Palace after V.C. Investiture, 1945. On right, Kitty Stephens.

Jack with Gunner.

(From left) Dave Blackie, Alf Messerug and Jack Hinton, Ohinemuri Races.

*(From left) Jack Hinton V.C., Vice Admiral B.C.G. Place V.C. and H.R.H.
Princess Anne, Cafe Royal 14 July 1972.*

*(Above) Jack meeting Fritz Hahn
for the first time in 48 years,
August, 1990. (Left) The prison at
Muhlhausen.*

(Above, from left) Bill Talbot, Jack Hinton, Harry Harrison, Doug Dalton, and Albre Petersen. (Below) Jack and Molly walking beside the Avon River near their Bexley home in Christchurch.

(From left) Charles Upham, Jack Hinton, Jim Burrows at the Bridge of Remembrance, Christchurch, 1989.

fence. In just one movement Jack stepped over the trip-wire and took a running jump at the fence. It was difficult to climb but somehow he made it up and over the top, with Dennis following. They climbed over the barbed wire entanglements and scaled the overhang and dropped silently on to the road outside the camp. They had made it! Jack expected to hear the shouts of the guards at any minute, but amazingly none came. Even the Alsatian dogs guarding the camp were quiet – luck seemed to be on their side.

They ran down the road as fast as they could. There was a forest at the end of the road. They would stand more of a chance once they were in the safety of the forest. It was then that Jack discovered that Dennis was no good in the dark.

"I can't see where I'm going!" he called to Jack.

"Why the hell didn't you tell me this before?" asked Jack, exasperated.

"Keep as close to me as possible!" he called to Dennis.

Jack slowed down, reasoning that the forest provided them with good cover. It was getting late, and it was unlikely that their disappearance would be discovered until next day at the earliest. The others would cover for them as long as they possibly could.

It was pitch dark and eerie in the forest, and because there was no light at all they had no idea in which direction to head. They kept close together and hoped for the best. Eventually after about an hour's walk, they saw a glimmer of light ahead.

"It must be the town ahead" Jack said to Dennis. They inched forward, as quietly as possible. Just then an owl hooted close by, making the men jump in fright. At almost the same time the moon came out from behind a dark cloud, revealing the outline of a railway line. They could see several wagons loaded with big boulders. With any luck the train would move off soon. Jack and Dennis looked around quickly and then climbed into one of the wagons and lay down in one corner each. Each man hoped the boulders would camouflage their bodies. Suddenly they heard a whistle being blown and felt the train start to move off. It was cramped in the wagon and the cold night air pierced through the men's clothes. But they were free! So far so good. The train continued on its journey, destination unknown. Jack whispered to

Dennis that as soon as it came to a halt they would have to make a break for it. About half an hour later the train came to a shuddering stop. Gingerly the two men stepped out of the wagon, thankful that the night was so dark. The train had pulled up in a big marshalling yard. They decided to stretch their legs. Jack walked ahead, expecting Dennis to follow. After he had gone a few paces, he called softly behind him:

"Shake it up, Den!"

There was no answer from Dennis.

"What the hell are you doing, Den?" said Jack, wondering what had happened.

He was answered by a guttural voice in German.

"Vott!"

Jack almost jumped out of his skin. They had been discovered. What rotten luck, and where on earth was Dennis?

–10–
IF AT FIRST...

"FORTUNE FAVOURS THE AUDACIOUS"
- ERASMUS -

Jack's heart pounded in his chest. How had they been discovered? Wait a minute – maybe they hadn't been. Quick as a flash and almost without thinking, he answered in a loud clear voice: "Nichts" (Nothing). There was no reply and Jack carried on walking.

After a few paces he heard footsteps behind him. Was the German following him? He started to break into a run, when suddenly a hand was clamped on his shoulder. Jack was just about to swing a punch when a voice said: "Hey! Steady on! It's me." It was Dennis.

Dennis told Jack that he had started to follow him after they had left the train, but had seen the German train worker. He had hung back hoping that Jack would not run into him. All had gone well until Jack had called out.

The two men decided to climb back on board the train and they made for a nearby wagon. As Dennis started to climb into the wagon after Jack, he slipped and his foot was caught between the rails. He tried to pull his foot out but it was stuck fast. He was desperate in case someone should see him, and also there was the fear that the train might move.

"Hurry, Den!" said Jack urgently.

"I can't – my bloody foot's stuck!"

Dennis gave one last heave and his foot moved a little. In desperation, he bent down and pulled his foot out of the boot.

He jumped into the wagon after Jack just as it was starting to move off. The wagon was full of coils of electric cables, and the men tried to make themselves as comfortable as possible.

131

For the rest of that night and all through the next day the train sped through Germany. There were no more opportunities to get off the train, and they simply had to stick it out. They had no food other than a chocolate bar each and a flask of water that they had smuggled out of camp. They were careful to make their supply last.

Early in the morning of the second day, they were awakened abruptly when their wagon was shunted backwards into a siding. Their train had smashed into another wagon. The end of their wagon was badly damaged and Jack and Dennis were shaken up. Just then the sliding door to their wagon was opened and a railway guard, in the company of some workers, appeared at the door. When they saw Jack and Dennis they were so astonished they could hardly speak.

There was no alternative but to surrender.

They got shakily to their feet. In the company of some German guards they were taken to a civilian jail, after much discussion in German, where they were thrown into the cells. For some time they were left alone, but later in the day they were given a thorough search and interrogation by trained Gestapo.

"Who are you?" they demanded harshly, "and what were you doing on the train?"

"I am required to give you only my name, rank and serial number." said Jack. Which he did.

"Do you take us for fools?" said one of the interrogators. "You are spies."

Jack repeated his name, rank and serial number and professed ignorance of all other matters. He and Dennis were asked about underground organisations and who had helped them. Their repeated replies were always negative, so finally they were passed on to the search guard.

Both men had to stand in the centre of a white circle and disrobe. Their clothes were thrown into the centre of a long table where white-smocked and gloved agents ripped out the linings and seams, and then pulled the soles and heels off their boots. While this was taking place, other agents searched their ears, noses, eyes and mouths.

The men were then returned to their cells for the rest of the day. That evening the interrogation started again. Who helped you? What are your real names? What were you really doing on the train? Etc. etc.

"My name is Jack Hinton" said Jack wearily. "I am a New Zealander and my serial number..." Before he could finish what he was saying, a savage blow was delivered to his kidneys. The sheer force of it knocked him over. In his weakened state he lay on the floor for a few moments, the breath momentarily knocked out of him.

"You are a British spy!" screamed the German. "We will get the truth out of you!"

Dennis was dragged off to another room and Jack was left on his own. He sat on the floor and wondered what he should do. He had had no food for several days and very little water. He knew he was in a precarious position. If they didn't believe his and Dennis's stories, they could languish in jail for weeks, maybe months. He had heard stories in camp about what the Gestapo did to escaped prisoners. They did not give a damn for the Geneva Convention. He felt his frustration build into a rage. He thought back to an incident that had happened to a friend of his, Tom Hurapapara from the 28th Maori Battalion. Hurapapara had also served in World War I. He had escaped from Molsdorf and when caught he had been interrogated by the Gestapo and had been savagely beaten up. He had been taunted by the thug who beat him, calling him "Schwarzer".

Within an hour a guard appeared and pushed Jack into a cell. The cell was dirty and tiny, the only light coming from a small window high up in the wall. On the floor were mattresses made of straw. These were flea-infested and placed on double-decker wooden bunks. There were no blankets.

A small figure, a Serb with a hard wracking cough and wearing filthy ragged clothes, sat in one corner. In the other corner was a Belgian, equally dirty and pathetic-looking. All through the night Jack stayed awake, unable to sleep on the hard mattress, his thoughts in turmoil, and listening to the coughing and moans of the other prisoners when they turned over in their sleep.

In the morning half a loaf of stale black bread was passed to the men through a grille in the door. The Belgian made a dive for the bread, almost knocking over a pitcher of water which had been roughly pushed into their hands. The Belgian then drank thirstily, passing the pitcher to Jack, after rubbing the edge of his filthy shirt over the rim. The pathetic little Serb did not move.

About two hours later, to Jack's amazement a face appeared at the grille in the door. It was a young Frenchman who handed the men half a cabbage and some bread. The men ate ravenously as the Frenchman explained that he wanted whatever they could spare which he could pass on to the underground escape organisation.

In the afternoon the air in the cell became more rancid and cold. The little Serb began to shiver uncontrollably. Jack took off his jacket and put it over the huddled figure. The shivering ceased for a while.

Around 8 o'clock that evening, Jack awoke from an uneasy doze to find a burly German standing over him. He was pulled roughly to his feet and shoved out of the cell and along a dingy grimy corridor. There was a door at one end. The German pushed him through it, and he was half thrown on to a chair in front of a desk. The room was dark, the only light coming from a naked bulb swinging from the ceiling. Beyond the desk, half hidden in the dark, a small, slightly-built man wearing an expensive dark pin-striped suit, bent over a pile of papers. A half-smoked cigarette lay burning in an ash tray in front of him.

The burly German withdrew, leaving Jack sitting in the chair. For a moment or two there was silence. The man behind the desk kept on writing, the scratching of his pen the only sound in the small dark room. Jack wondered what was going to happen, and his stomach turned over in anticipation.

Suddenly the man looked up, and as he did so the sudden movement cast a light on his face. It was a narrow face, the light blue eyes hidden by pince-nez. Jack noted the sparse fair hair, the immaculate hands and finger nails, the cuticles even and pushed back.

The man got up from behind the desk and stood in front of

Jack. He leaned against the desk.

"Awfully sorry old man to keep you waiting," he said. "You must think me impolite – pressure of work, I'm afraid."

The accent was English, with a slight trace of German. Jack must have shown his surprise, for the man said: "My name is Hauptmann Greiner, Chief Gestapo Officer of the district. I studied in England before the war – your Oxford – a beautiful place, don't you think, old man?"

"No, I don't know. Never been to the bloody place," said Jack. "And don't call me 'old man'!"

His outburst did not seem to faze Greiner at all. His expression never altered. Instead, he went back to his desk and reached into a drawer. He pulled out a packet of cigarettes.

"Awfully sorry, old man – would you like a cigarette?" Jack didn't budge. He certainly had no intention of taking anything from him.

"You know what you can do with your precious cigarette," he told Greiner, with a bravado he did not feel. Greiner's features hardened slightly.

"I hope you won't be foolish" he said. "If you are sensible we can get this whole unpleasant business over as quickly as possible."

He took a puff from the cigarette lying in the ashtray.

"Now tell me your correct name, which country you are spying for, and the names of your friends who have helped you." "I'll tell you bastards nothing," Jack spat out, thinking of the pitiful sights in his cell – the small huddled figure of the Serb and the starved and beaten Belgian.

"I see you have decided to be foolish after all," said Greiner. "It is a pity. We could get along well if you co-operate with us. We will give you an excellent meal, wine, and a decent bed to sleep in, We will find out everything in the end, anyway. I must tell you that your friend has decided to tell us everything. It did not take us long to learn all we needed to know."

"If you know so bloody much, what are you asking me for?" said Jack.

This logic infuriated the German. He pressed a small buzzer hidden under his desk.

135

"I don't think you will find it so funny in front of Hans," he said.

The door suddenly opened and a huge man, twice the size of Greiner, came into the room. His shirt sleeves were rolled up to his elbows and there was an ugly scar down his right cheek. He stood in front of Jack, so close that he could smell the stale beer on his breath. He stood for a moment looking down at Jack, then suddenly he hit him as hard as he could across the head. The force of the blow knocked Jack off the chair. Pain and fury replaced his fear, and his boxing training came to the fore. He let fly with a right cross, catching the thug off balance and knocking him over. Greiner pressed the buzzer under his desk again and swiftly two guards rushed into the room. They gripped Jack by both his arms as the burly thug leapt to his feet with a snarl.

When he woke up he was on the floor of his cell. His body was wracked with pain, and the cold of the hard ground seeped into his aching bones. He tried to rouse himself, but even the smallest effort made him want to cry out with pain. His ribs must be broken, he thought. He put a finger up to his face, touching it gently. It was covered in blood. A great pain seared through his nose, his cheek and his head. I wonder if my nose is broken, he thought. He noticed he was alone except for the Belgian. There was no sign of the pathetic little Serb. The Belgian came over to him.

"I see they got you too," he said.

"Don't try and move. I'll get water for you."

With some difficulty the Belgian managed to get Jack on to his bunk. He told Jack that the Serb had been taken away, probably for good. He held some water to Jack's parched lips. He sipped it gratefully. His head felt as if it was on fire. He lay back on the bed and tried to sleep.

It seemed as if he had only just gone to sleep, but in fact it was several hours later when he was sent for again. He was roughly propelled along the dusty passageway again, every movement agonising. He was shoved into the same room, and into the same chair in front of the desk where Hauptmann Greiner sat.

"You'd better warn your henchman that if I get him, I'll kill him," said Jack.

"So, you are not afraid" said Greiner. "I admire your plucki-
ness. But we are here to ascertain certain facts. I will ask you once
again. Where were you going when you were arrested, and who
helped you?"

"My name is Jack Hinton and my rank is Sergeant, New
Zealand Army. My serial number is 7930. I am a prisoner-of-war
and the Geneva Convention states that you have to honour its
terms regarding prisoners," said Jack.

"Come, come," said Greiner. "You surely don't expect me to
believe that you are a prisoner-of-war. The Geneva Convention
does not interest me in the slightest."

"That would be typical, coming from swine like you!" said
Jack.

Greiner picked up a fountain pen from his desk and held it
between both his fingers. He studied it carefully.

"I will ask you once more. What are the names of your friends,
what is your business, and which country are you spying for?"

"If you check at my camp, you will soon discover I am telling
you the truth, you stupid bastard!" said Jack. A guard was
standing in one corner of the room and now he made a move
towards Jack, but Greiner motioned him to stay put. Instead
surprisingly, he came from behind his desk and offered Jack a
cigarette once again. Jack's first instinct was to refuse again, but
he thought "What the hell," and took the cigarette and put it in
his mouth.

"We will, of course, check up on your story" said Greiner,
lighting Jack's cigarette with a lighter. "If I find you have been
lying to me you will be sorry."

"Not half as sorry as you will be when this war finishes" said
Jack.

"I would warn you very strongly to curb your insolence," said
Greiner threateningly. "Remember no one knows where you are.
People disappear all the time."

Something in the German's tone filled Jack with sudden fear.
He mustn't do anything stupid. What had happened to Dennis,
and would he see him again? He was taken back to his cell, where
for the next two days he nursed his injuries. His only companion

137

was the quiet little Belgian. All they had to look forward to was their daily diet of black bread and water. Early in the morning of the third day Jack awoke to find another figure had been tossed into his cell. It was Dennis! Dennis's face was black and blue, and he was hardly recognisable. The two men greeted each other joyfully, and Dennis told Jack his story. He had suffered virtually the same treatment as Jack. He had not told the Germans any more than Jack had.

On the fourth day Jack and Dennis were brought before Greiner again.

"So! We have checked your story. It would seem you have been telling me the truth after all. How did you get out of this prison?" he asked Jack.

"We walked out of the main gate when we went to the toilet," said Jack.

"You with the V.C. – you wouldn't tell lies, would you?"

"I never told a lie in my life!" said Jack.

"It is lucky for you that you have not made any trouble while you have been here," said Greiner, looking directly at Jack. And then at the guard:

"Schick diese zwei Idioten fort von hier! Schicke die Wachter hinein!" (Get these two idiots out of here. Send in the guards!)

The next minute two guards from Molsdorf arrived and they were escorted back to camp. Amazingly Jack and Dennis had not been missed until the Gestapo had notified the camp, as their fellow prisoners had covered for them very well. Jack and Dennis were given 21 days solitary for escaping, but first they had to be deloused. They stripped and were sprayed with a disinfectant, while their dirty clothes were put into the delousing chamber. Then they showered and dried themselves while they waited for their clothes to be returned. They were then given a bowl of watery soup and three slices of bread – their daily ration. The two men were ravenous and they fell on the food.

Jack's sentence for escaping was deferred because the whole camp was shortly to be moved to a new prison building in Muhlhausen. One day soon after Jack had returned from the jail, he and the other men were marching around the compound singing "Marschieren für Deutschland" (Marching on Germany). The camp Kommandant took a dim view of this, and told the men that they were not allowed to sing that song. One bright spark asked if they could whistle it instead. That seemed to go down all right with the Kommandant!

Quite often the Kommandant would go over to Hut 13 to hear the BBC news, and to find out how the war was progressing. He had even given the prisoners maps and flags as he was interested to see how far the Russians were advancing.

One time all the prisoners went on strike because they were tired of the starvation diet – they wanted two kartoffelen a day instead of the one they were receiving. The whole camp sat on its backside in the compound, and nothing would shift them. They refused to do any cleaning and the guards had no choice but to clean the camp themselves! They took off their side arms while they cleaned the yard and put the rubbish in the wagons. While they did this Dennis and Jack, out of sight of the guards, took their belts and bayonets and put them down the latrines.

When the guards had finished their work they looked for their guns but to no avail. When the Kommandant heard what happened, he ordered that all the huts were to be thoroughly searched. Finally the latrines were searched, and the guns were discovered. Two guards were then ordered to go down in the latrines up to their waists and then clean the guns with buckets of water in front of the jeers of all the prisoners!

On 20 September, 1943 the whole camp was moved in box-cars to a new prison building in Muhlhausen, Thuringen. Muhlhausen was near Leipzig in East Germany and was called Zweilager, also the Castle on the hill. Muhlhausen had been an old brewery prior to the war, and the prisoners were told that it was escape-proof and was for criminal prisoners only, like Jack.

At the station they were met by large bodies of guards and police and were marched under escort to their new quarters about two kilometres away. The camp was on a slight rise, and at first sight was very different from the usual compounds. It was a large building, more like a jail, and was the Germans' answer to the many escapes and tunnels built at Molsdorf.

At the entrance to the camp were huge gates which led into a cobblestone courtyard. Jack lined up with the other 500 or so men for the never-ending head count. They were assigned to a dormitory which could hold about twelve men in double-decked bunks. There were two floors, as well as cells in the dungeons, which were dark, damp and flea-infested. It soon became apparent to Jack that Muhlhausen would be difficult to escape from.

There was plenty of room and Jack shared an upstairs room with just four other men. Opposite the prison was an empty paddock where some of the prisoners were allowed to go each day for recreation. Some Kiwis, Canadians, English and Scots obtained a football through the Red Cross. They managed to get a couple of teams together to play rugby. The guards had no idea how the game was played, and they thought the men were mad when they saw them tackling one another. The men usually played together about twice a week.

One day soon after Jack had entered Muhlhausen, he was told he had to serve his 21 days solitary confinement. He was led to an underground cell, about 4 metres x 2 metres, with a small barred window high up on the wall. There was a wooden bunk, but no mattress, pillow or blankets. The solid cell door had a "glass eye" where the guards would check on him every so often. The only source of heat came from a small wood stove outside the cell door. Very little daylight filtered in from the small window as the cell was underground. It was always cold in the cell even on the odd occasion when the stove was burning. Owing to the solidly-constructed door little heat was unable to penetrate.

One guard, who Jack and the others had nicknamed "Plankface" for obvious reasons visited the solitary cells four times a day. Plankface was only an Obergefreiter, a slight step above a lance-corporal. He was a died-in-the-wool Nazi and a member of the party. All the other guards, and even the Kommandant seemed to fear him.

Plankface was about 2 metres tall with thin stooped shoulders. His whole body was angular and bony. His eyes were sunken and baleful and they were set in a skull-like face. His cheeks were hollow and the long etched creased lines extended down to the corners of his lips, pulling his mouth down into a perpetual surly expression. He was not a pretty sight. He would usually arrive in the morning with a jug of water and three slices of black bread. He was inclined to rant and rave at the slightest provocation and Jack and some of the Canadian prisoners who had befriended him, like big Bob Prouse who had been captured at Dieppe, usually went out of their way to annoy Plankface. They were certain he was a Nazi stooge and informer.

Prouse, nicknamed "Mickey" or "Minnie" after the famous Disney mouse characters, to rhyme with Prouse, was also doing solitary for laughing at the camp Kommandant and for smoking a cigarette on morning roll-call. Prouse had been a military policeman before the war.

On his first day in solitary Prouse had managed to smear the "glass eye" in the cell door by wetting his finger and rubbing it on the walls of the cell, thus coating it with whitewash. Plankface ranted and raved at Prouse who pretended he didn't understand what he was on about. He tried to catch Prouse out at what he was doing, but to no avail. He finally gave up. Knowing he was outside Prouse would yell at him: "Hello Plankface, you ugly bastard, how are you today?"

Plankface would go rushing in and say in German, "What is Plankface?"

And Prouse would reply: "Nicht verstehen!"

They hated each other's guts.

Jack was taken out of his cell three times a day. In the morning he would be taken to the latrines and then to the washroom where he would be locked in for 15 minutes to wash and shave. Somehow he would always manage a quick smoke from butts that had been hidden in the ashes of the boilers by other prisoners. When he got his half-hour exercise in the afternoon he would walk with his hand behind his back.

One morning when Prouse was in solitary he heard a voice calling his name. He heard the voice again. It was very faint and at first he thought it was his imagination, but it continued and he tried to find out where it was coming from. Finally, he traced it

141

to a small iron plate on the cell wall, and, by tugging and pulling, he was able to remove the plate to reveal a cleaned-out space. The voice became clearer and when he put his ear to the space he could hear quite well.

It was Jack. Jack told him to hold his hand in the hole with palm up. Prouse did so, and within seconds, a cigarette dropped into his palm, followed by a match. Jack was in the cell above Prouse, which had a stove-pipe inside it. By removing the clean-out plate from the pipe, Jack could put his hand in the opening, and flick the cigarette past the elbow and into the flue, where it dropped into Prouse's cell.

Jack had received the cigarettes from some of his friends, who bribed one of the friendly guards to pass them along. The cigarettes were a godsend to Prouse, but he had to blow the smoke into the flue, smoke the cigarette as low as possible, and then grind the remains into the soot. Even with these precautions, Plankface would come in, sniff the air and accuse Prouse of smoking. He would just shrug as Plankface searched him and the cell. He never did discover the method, so he couldn't charge him, which would have meant an additional seven days confinement.

Jack felt a great affinity with the Canadian POWs. They were great comrades in prison life. Besides Bob Prouse who came from Ontario, there was Edward Heath from Oakville, and Spike Wallace from Saskatchewan. The Canadians were also generous and shared their booty of cigarettes and other goods from the Red Cross parcels which were few and far between for New Zealand and Australian prisoners. Their generosity was something Hinton had not experienced previously with his British compatriots in prison camp. The Canadian Red Cross parcels contained Klim milk powder, coffee, tea, cigarettes, chocolates, and clothing such as long johns.

One day they mixed a batch of alcohol homebrew made out of raisins, prunes, and apples in an athletics storage closet in Muhlhausen. After months of waiting a small group of POWs including Heath and Hinton, decided it was high time to crack it open. But no sooner were they tasting their homebrew, than an air raid siren sounded to send all the men downstairs to shelter.

Despite the threat of discovery by German soldiers who searched every room following an air raid, Jack refused to leave the homebrew. Upon his return, the first thing Heath saw was Jack Hinton, V.C. stripped to the waist with his pants rolled up to his knees standing on the table doing a war dance. And across the room sat a German soldier, half-undressed and three-parts drunk, with his rifle in the corner.

Edward Heath had first met Jack in Molsdorf in 1942. Heath had also been one of the 2,000 Canadian troops of the ill-fated Dieppe raid. The two men almost naturally gravitated together, sharing a zest for sports. Heath was on the sports committee. He, like Jack, had a disdain for the military discipline of the British High Command. He always maintained that they were there to fight a war, not to shine shoes. The two men also shared a common delight in harassing their German guards by escaping.

Heath, who himself made three escape attempts, including one with 51 other POWs through the tunnel at Molsdorf, believed that it was the duty of every POW to attempt to escape. If they were not escaping, they were causing havoc. It was a major offence to steal from a mate, but you could steal anything from the Germans. With all the problems they caused, the Germans didn't know which way to turn.

Plankface alternated with another guard. He was named Fritz Hahn and had been shot up on the Russian Front. He had been wounded in the head and arms. Hahn lived in Eisenberg, East Germany, and took considerable risks for Jack. The two became quite friendly. Hahn was also an artist and used to while away the time doing sketches.

Hahn advised Jack not to cross Plankface as he was considered a dangerous man. While Jack was in solitary Hahn would take him out to the latrines during the night and he would give Jack a mug of ersatz coffee which was putrid, a cigarette, and sometimes an apple or a piece of white bread. It was Fritz who had told Jack that Bob Prouse was in the cell directly below him.

Jack settled back into the routine of camp life after serving his 21 days solitary. Time passed slowly. Most of the time it was boring and discouraging, but what made it possible to endure was the wonderful comradeship and unselfishness of most of the other prisoners. They were bound together by deprivation and hardship. On Saturday nights there was usually a concert or a boxing match.

The trumpeter in the camp band was a talented and amusing man who kept the whole camp alive and laughing. He chose his music with care as the song titles conveyed hidden messages. Some examples were: "The love bug will get you" (Medical Officer inspection for vermin), "Don't tie my hands, let me wander" (chains on Canadians a.m.), "Deepest shelter in town" (air raid/ to shelters), "A hunting we will go" (Gestapo search), "Hold your hand out, you naughty boy" (camp punishment), "Oh you nasty man" (when the Jerry known as 'Double Amp' was near), and "Let's put out the lights and go to sleep" (lights out, 10pm).

The trumpet was just one method of passing on news. The men just lived for rumours and the favourite sayings were: "What's the griff?" or, "What's the latest? If the news was encouraging, the men would be elated for days on end. If it was bad, when the tides of war reversed against the Allies, the prisoners suffered with them, and fell into fits of depression. Most of the time the men bounced back – after all they had their mates to bolster them up.

Each day a British NCO would visit each room and call out, "News time". He was the runner who would bring them the latest word from the BBC. They never knew where the wireless was located, how it was obtained, or who operated it, but they were always grateful for the service. They would also get information from men sent to town to unload railway wagons, who would then have quiet conversations with the French train engineers. Scraps of information came from prisoners transferred from other camps also.

They heard stories of men in work camps deliberately placing their lives and their health at risk. They heard how one man put his hand on a rock in a stone quarry and persuaded another man to chop his fingers off so he could go to hospital. They learned of men shot for trying to escape. They learned that the war in the Western Desert was at last being won by the Allies, and also of the mass murder of Polish officers in Katyn Woods.

The men held auctions where cigarettes or prison money served as cash. A bar of chocolate would bring 200 cigarettes, soap went for 50 and toothpaste or shoe polish would go for 100 cigarettes each. The highest-priced item was a quarter-pound of tea. At one auction this brought 500 Reich marks in POW money, equivalent to about 150 Canadian dollars.

Jack found the Germans either resourceful, or very stupid and single-minded. For example, during the constant Gestapo searches, if they were looking for knives, they would ignore some other forbidden item. One day, during a surprise search, they came running in looking for guns. One of the Canadians was lying on his bed looking over his map, trying to figure out which way to go on some future escape. The Gestapo threw the map to the floor and proceeded to slit his palliasse wide open, strewing the straw everywhere. They tore the place apart, but left the map lying on the floor. This search would have been unsuccessful if it hadn't been for the fact that one of the accompanying guards walked across the courtyard and, in ducking under the line of underwear and socks hanging in the yard, he banged his head in a sock with a pistol concealed in the toe. He rubbed his head and continued on his way. All of a sudden he stopped as it gradually dawned on him that a sock should not be so hard. He was the hero of the day and the whole camp was put on strafe (punishment).

Very few of the guards could give an order quietly. They had to scream their instructions if an order was not carried out to their satisfaction. They would shout continuously "Raus" (short for "heraus") and "Schnell machen" (Get out and make it fast). The prisoners would mutter "Fuck off" in response!

Most of the prisoners in Muhlhausen found the weekends to be the worst, especially Sundays, as the German soldiers would invariably walk their girls past the building. The girls would look up at the prisoners watching them through the bars and flirt openly. The men would start a chorus of wolf-whistles which would enrage their escorts and the girls would be hurried away. Although the men would laugh, the sight of the pretty girls would only increase their loneliness.

On New Year's Day, 1944, hundreds of planes passed over Muhlhausen Camp and the air-raid sirens began to wail. Jack heard the sound of machine-gun fire as the fighters engaged in dog-fights. All the prisoners were herded immediately into the shelters. As the shelters were riddled with thousands of fleas it was a miserable way to herald the start of 1944.

As the New Year progressed the raids became more and more frequent and continued on throughout the spring. Seldom a day passed without the sirens forcing the men down to the shelters. Jack often felt the whole camp shudder as a disabled bomber would jettison its bombs in a nearby field.

In early April, 1944 word came through the grapevine that 76 Royal Air Force officers had made a mass escape from Stalag Luft III. They had escaped in March and later they heard that 50 of the prisoners had been shot and killed after recapture. The Germans stated that some of the men had tried to resist recapture and others had tried to re-escape while being transported back to the prison camp. These were German lies to cover up mass murder. What the men did not know then was that Hitler had issued an order on 4 March 1944 named "Bullet Decree" which stated in part that recaptured prisoners, "other than British or American" were to be turned over to the Sicherheitsdienst (Security Service) for execution.

It was always on the cards that escaped prisoners could be shot. However, it was a risk that Jack was prepared to take. It was a strong likelihood, especially if caught by the SS or Hitler Youth fanatics, but he dismissed it from his mind and honestly felt that it would never happen to him.

On 6 June, 1944, the Allies invaded Normandy in France. At last the end of the war was in sight. The men at Muhlhausen heard at noon about the 6.00am landing. It was a moment of great rejoicing. Before D-Day they had despaired that freedom would never come, but once this happened they knew they would be alright. Jack and his friends were so thrilled that they feasted on prunes that they had been hoarding and smoked precious English cigarettes rather recklessly. Every British soldier was smiling but the German sentries were glum and depressed.

In July, Jack and the others received news over the shortwave set that Anthony Eden, in a recent speech, had condemned the Germans for murdering escaping POWs. The German answer was to post a notice on their bulletin board stating that German civilians would shoot to kill any escaping prisoners in revenge for the heavy bombing of their cities. The very next day they heard that two prisoners had been killed for assaulting a guard and two others while attempting to escape. It would seem that the Germans were getting jumpy with the incessant bombing and the fact that the Allies were starting to win the war.

Another notice went up stating that they would be shot without any warning if they left their rooms at night or stepped over the trip-wire in the daytime. On 10 September as the air raids continued bombs fell on the town of Muhlhausen, killing 10 civilians. On the 12th more bombs hit the town and 30 more were killed. Giving the heavy bombing as a reason, the Germans cut their Red Cross parcels to half a parcel a week. The prisoners took this to be good news. The planes were hitting their depots and marshalling yards.

As the weeks progressed more POWs were killed while attempting to escape from one of the work camps and evacuees were pouring into Muhlhausen from other towns. Another notice was posted on the bulletin board stating that if escaping prisoners were caught in civilian clothing they would be shot immediately as bandits, spies or saboteurs.

During the month of November the bombing raids became so frequent that the prisoners spent more time in the shelters than in the camp itself. By this time they searched for new hiding places as the dungeons were becoming unendurable. On 1 December a whole room of 12 men received twenty-one days strafe for not retreating to the shelters. There was no doubt that the Allies were getting closer every day. Jack's main concern was to stay alive until he was freed. On 14 December they were ordered to draw the remainder of their Red Cross parcels from storage and were advised that there would be no more issues as Geneva was completely out of them. The bombing of depots and trains was again given as the reason. It looked as if it was going to be a poor

Christmas and a hungry winter!

Christmas Day, 1944, was Jack's fourth Christmas as a POW. He hoped it would be his last. On the 27th one of the men was found dead in his bunk. He was one of the Dunkirk men, and after so long in captivity, his heart finally failed.

During January there was some respite from the bombing raids, but in February they started again. One day during a particularly heavy raid, Jack was part of the group of a wood party which went out two or three times a week to dig up stumps from a forest about four kilometres from the camp. They were on an honours system not to escape as the wood was for their own benefit. There was now no firewood at all left in the camp. The best part of the trip was the noon break, when the guards wanted to eat their lunch and have a beer in nearby Peterhof, a guest house. They couldn't leave the prisoners unguarded, so they took them in the back door, where they had the use of a separate room and were able to buy beer by bribing the guards with cigarettes.

On their way back to camp Jack heard the noise of approaching bombers again, and they started to run with the guards to the nearest air raid shelter. Adults were also running with their children. One woman beckoned Jack and asked him to look after her little "kinder". He scooped up the child and ran towards the nearest shelter. As he did so bombs started to fall, creating large craters in the ground. Finally he reached the shelter in safety together with the other POWs. The civilians who were in the shelter were amazed to see the children with the prisoners. There were some Russians outside the shelter trying to get in but they were not allowed. When Jack went outside after the raid was over, he was distressed to see the bodies of the Russians strewn around like rag dolls. They had had no chance.

One day the SS came around to the camp and lined a group of men up against the brick wall of the building. One of these men was Mervyn Wallace from Jack's 20 Battalion. They hit Wallace viciously in the face and sent him reeling back on to the wall. Jack is sure this was done to let the prisoners know they were still in charge. One French man in the camp stole an egg one day and was sent to a Special Camp (Sonderlager) for six weeks. When he returned he was skin and bone.

There was death all round Jack. The town of Muhlhausen suffered another direct hit and nearby Gotha was heavily damaged with over 400 killed, including 11 more POWs.

On 1 February martial law was declared and the feeling in the camp was one of exhilaration, knowing that the end was not too far away. There was a continuous stream of prisoners on the march, from Poland and Eastern Germany, as the Germans fell back from the Russian advance. The sick prisoners, unable to go any further, were dropped off at the already overcrowded camp. Trucks arrived at the camp daily filled with pitiful human beings piled high like lengths of wood. The camp doctor and medics did their best with the meagre supplies available, but in many cases it was hopeless.

By March the camp population had swollen to more than 1,000. It was full of lice brought in by the daily arrivals, and on 19 March Jack received an anti-typhus injection. On the 21st there was a further cut to the rations. The prisoners now received a 2 kilo loaf of bread between 9 men per day.

The guards were trigger-happy now that the end was in sight. Some prisoners were shot for the slightest reason and for disobeying orders. Jack could hear the sound of machine-gun fire constantly, and he knew the Allies could not be far away. He knew that he must stay alive now and hang on.

He learned that typhus had broken out in his old camp of Stalag IXC in Bad Sulza. The heavy raids continued during the night and in the distance he could see the glow of flames lighting up the sky over Eisenach. The sound of guns was getting closer and closer. The following morning, 2 April, he was rudely awakened and told they were all going to evacuate the camp. Jack had considered the possibility of this happening so decided to feign sickness so he would be left behind with the sick and wounded.

While the others were preparing to leave he went down to the cellars and hid. He waited a long time and then went upstairs and found most of the prisoners, and all the guards, had gone. In the guardroom on the wall he found a bunch of keys to the gates, so he pocketed them. He still has these keys to this day. It was then he heard gunfire. He climbed up a lookout tower and looked down on a fierce battle. An American armoured division and infantry had attacked from the west and east. The Germans were completely bowled over and houses were set on fire. Anti-tank shells scorched the air.

Jack headed off through the gates of Muhlhausen and on to the road. He was free at last! He cast a look back at the camp for the last time. The roads were crowded with endless streams of civilians, evacuees from the bombed cities, carrying bundles and suitcases or pushing prams and carts containing all their worldly belongings. Along the sides of the roads were burned-out German tanks, scout cars and trucks – all victims of the air raids. Diving planes machine-gunned all moving vehicles, freight trains and railway depots.

Jack was nearly at the end of the German lines when he suddenly saw an American tank coming towards him. Two men in American uniform were standing in the turret, semi-automatic Garand rifles slung over their shoulders. He waved to them enthusiastically and ran forward towards them.

"Not so fast, buddy" drawled a mid-West American accent.

"No God-damned Kraut gets past us alive."

–11–
GOIN' HOME, MATE

"IT IS NOT RIGHT TO EXALT OVER SLAIN MEN"
– HOMER –

Jack pulled up abruptly before a platoon of the American 6 Armoured Division. He had rushed forward to greet the Americans with a feeling of exhilaration and excitement. However instead of a welcome, the Americans had challenged him with suspicion. They demanded to see his identification and searched him from head to foot, looking for hidden weapons.

He was taken to a temporary headquarters set up by the Americans, where he was interrogated for two hours. The Americans were taking no chances. The roads were full of escaping Germans wearing civilian clothes who were trying to evade capture at all costs. Luckily for Jack they believed his story, for he had left his identification disks behind at the camp. The Americans allowed him to borrow an American uniform, then he went forward with the Fourty-Fourth Infantry Division. He took part in brief actions while they captured three more villages. White flags flew from almost every building and window. Jack could hear small bursts of sporadic gunfire as the odd pocket of resistance was cleared out.

There was chaos everywhere. Jack helped round up German prisoners, most of them giving up quietly. After being a POW for so long Jack had often wondered what he would feel when the tables were turned. Now he felt nothing but compassion for one poor German soldier, as he gave himself up. He saw the fear in his eyes and his hands shook as he showed Jack photos of his wife and two children. Why couldn't his first prisoners have been ratbags like Plankface?

Many German women were zealous in their efforts to please

the Americans, and they were more than anxious to accommo-
date them as far as personal favours went. They lived in constant
fear of the advancing Russian army who raped and pillaged as
they went through Germany.

On 11 April Muhlhausen Camp was liberated by the Americans. Two American infantrymen walked in through the gates and
said: "Well boys, you're free!"

As most of the prisoners had been marched away a few days
before, there were only 225 left. They rushed out to greet the
Americans who showered the POWs with cigarettes and field
rations. One trooper even stripped off his battle jacket and
handed it to one of the Canadian prisoners. The officer in charge
laid out a map, asking directions and locations of other POW
camps. Those POWs who were fit enough helped to round up
Germans in the vicinity. They also received instructions from the
military authorities to stay close to the camp for their own safety.

In the meantime, Jack had fallen foul of an American colonel,
who for some reason or other was suspicious of Jack. When the
colonel found out that Jack was a New Zealander, he insisted on
him being interrogated again. This time the interrogation took
two days. The captain who interrogated Jack was under orders
to make absolutely certain that he was who he claimed to be. The
captain fired questions at him rapidly:

Number: 7930
Rank: Platoon Sergeant
Name: Hinton, John Daniel
Decorations: Victoria Cross
Were you wounded? Yes, through the stomach – 28 April, 1941
Unit: 20 Infantry Battalion
Date of birth: 17 September, 1909
Length of service: Since 5 October 1939
Peacetime occupation: Public Works Dept. Greymouth, N.Z.
Private address: C/- Mrs. H.G. Hinton, Colac Bay, Southland.
Did you carry any form of identification or photograph? Just a
paybook. I left my identification disk behind in Stalag IXC,
Muhlhausen, with friends. I joined up with an American platoon

belonging to 6 Armoured Div.
Do you speak any foreign language? No.

Jack was then evacuated through replacement channels for further interrogation before arrangements were finally made to transport him back to Britain with other POWs. He was then allowed a much-needed shower, given some U.S. dollars and two sergeants drove him in a German jeep across the Rhine to Belgium.

On the way they passed some British soldiers in a jeep. One of them yelled out to Jack: "Goin' home, mate?"

He was indeed, after an absence of nearly six years. At Namur, in Belgium, he caught a train to Brussels in the company of many other POWs and some German prisoners. On the train he sat quietly, trying to take in the fact that at long last he was free. It was a strange feeling. He looked out of the window at the night sky. It was full of vapour trails from the Air Forces still operating. He closed his eyes and listened to the noise of the train on the rails and the click of the wheels – clickety click, clickety click, getting nearer to home – home, every mile closer. It was a wonderful sound.

When he arrived at Brussels Jack and the other ex-POWs were given a mug of tea and delicious fruit cake, which he had not tasted for years, and biscuits. In a very short time the call came to board a Dakota. The DC3 had a crew of four who came from all corners of the Commonwealth. The seats were slung lengthways like an old-fashioned rail car. It was not long before he sighted England and the white cliffs of Dover.

It was the 12th of April and Jack landed on English soil for the first time in his life. The DC3 touched down at Wing in Buckinghamshire, north of London. The men were quickly sprayed with delousing powder, handed cigarettes and treated to a light supper served by WAAFs. The highlight of the meal was the white bread, which after Jack's long diet of black bread, looked and tasted like cake. That same night they were taken to a reception camp where the men were able to wash, eat a decent meal, issued with a new uniform, and go to bed.

At a reception for the returned men an Englishman went up to Jack and asked him: "How did you like those diced carrots we put in your parcels?" Jack answered: "It would have been better if you had put bloody meat in them instead!" Kip who was present said: "Come on! Let's get out of here quickly!" All Kiwi ex-POWs arriving back in England, were allocated to various "wings". These wings, all named after senior 2 NZEF officers – Freyberg, Puttick, Miles, Hargest, Barrowclough, Crump and Park – accommodated about 50 officers and a thousand men. Jack was sent to Puttick wing, Cliftonville, a suburb of Margate, in Kent. As well as the wings there was a Headquarters, which made up the 2 NZEF Reception Group. Major-General Howard Kippenberger, who had been severely wounded in Italy, had convalesced in England, and he was made Commander of the Reception Group. The wings were located in Folkestone, Cliftonville and Broadstairs, all in southern England, and there was a Group Hospital at Haine.

Puttick wing acted as a transit reception wing through which all repatriated POWs passed for preliminary equipping and processing before going to their permanent quarters. A club in London, the Fernleaf Club, in Knightsbridge, staffed by New Zealand Women's Army Auxiliary Corps personnel, was made available to all ex-Kiwi POWs. Howard Kippenberger broadcast a talk about the New Zealand Reception Group and said he was, "glad of an opportunity of being of service to so many old friends and comrades. All the time I intend to treat these men as soldiers. There will be discipline in the camps of a sort that, I think, will be calculated to maintain self-respect and to restore or keep high their morale."

All British ex-POWs were being flown to the United Kingdom at the rate of 10,000 or more a day. By the end of May more than 154,000 British Commonwealth (and there were 9,000 Kiwis) ex-POWs had landed on British soil. It was to be some time before transport was available to take the repatriated POWs home to New Zealand so provision was made to enable them to fill in the period of waiting. It was decided that each ex-POW would receive 28 days leave with 4s 6d a day subsistence allowance and a free railway warrant anywhere in the United Kingdom. They were also provided with occupations during this period to help them on the road to rehabilitation.

A complete Education and Rehabilitation Service in the United Kingdom was set up. In addition to the funds and goods supplied from the National Patriotic Fund, the Government passed a vote of 10,000 pounds to provide special comforts, entertainment, and conducted tours for ex-POWs during their stay.

As far back as October, 1944, the War Office had circularised all next-of-kin with a list of suggestions for handling their ex-POW relatives, based on ideas obtained from those already home. They emphasized the following points:

"Don't be hurt if he does not come and see you for a bit. Don't give him too much of a party when he does come to see you. Be a good listener...answer all his questions carefully.

Don't pity him. All he wants from friends and relatives is understanding help until he finds his feet."

Not long afterwards, similar advice was published in New Zealand.

Before going down to Margate, Jack went to London by train. As he came out of the railway station, he met two British soldiers. He didn't have a cent to his name, but he took them into a bar at the station. He asked the barmaid if they could have a sandwich and a beer each, but he had no money to pay for them. He told her he was a New Zealander. She told Jack in no uncertain terms that he certainly could not have anything without payment, so they went along the road and found a small pub. When he told the barmaid where he was from and what they wanted she told the men she had been to New Zealand and worked in Hamilton. She gave them beer and sandwiches without hesitation, and Jack told her to send the bill to the New Zealand High Commissioner, Bill Jordan. Later, when Jack arrived in Margate, he was told that he must not book up any more beers!

Jack stayed in London for a while and found the food

surprisingly good. Although food was in short supply, it was readily available to all ex-POWs. There was plenty of bread, eggs and bacon. After a short while Jack was surprised to find that the hunger craving quickly disappeared.

In the company of several other New Zealanders, Jack went to Margate by train. They took great delight in listening to the English voices, especially those of the children. They hadn't heard children speak for so long. On the train there were two children with their mother, chattering away. Suddenly they all went quiet. No one spoke, no one could handle it. After all they had gone through over the last five years – the death, destruction and deprivations, here were these children talking away excitedly with the innocence of youth. Jack found it very moving and emotionally disturbing.

Jack stayed at the Norfolk Hotel in Cliftonville, a suburb of Margate. He was just happy to sit in the sun. He had spent four long years as a prisoner. Now he could relax and try and repair his mind and body.

While at Margate he met up with three friends whom he had not seen for some time. They were three New Zealand doctors – Dr Lou Longmore, Dr Fred Moody, and Dr Selwyn De Clive Lowe.

Back in New Zealand Jack's mother, Mary, was thrilled to receive a telegram from Fred Jones, the Minister of Defence. The contents read as follows:

> Very pleased to inform you it is now reported that your son 7930 Sgt. John Daniel Hinton (V.C.) previously prisoner-of-war in Germany is now safe in United Kingdom (stop) The Prime Minister desires me to convey to you the Government's sincere pleasure at this good news and hopes that it will not be long before repatriation arrangements can be made.
>
> 15/4/45   F. JONES
Minister of Defence

On 7 May, 1945 at 0241 hours, the war in Europe officially

ended by the signing of the surrender document by Germany. The "war to end wars" as many historians have put it, lasted a little over 68 months. The surrender document ordered the simultaneous cessation of hostilities on all fronts on 8 May at 2301 hours. It confirmed the defeat of the armed forces of the Third Reich, and settled the procedure for their surrender.

Jack was in London for Victory in Europe Day, or V.E. Day as it was known. The streets of London were alive with celebrations. Thousands celebrated with uninhibited abandon. People danced in the streets and rejoiced in the fact that their loved ones had come home, or would soon be coming home. Bells rang across the city, and Union Jacks flew from buildings, and on statues and lampposts. Soldiers, sailors and airmen hugged and kissed any girl they could find. There were parties in the streets and tables laden with food. Everybody had saved rations for this momentous occasion.

Jack was caught up in the wild excitement and celebrations. However, there were times when the knowledge that the war was finally at an end took some time to sink in. As a prisoner-of-war he had so long lived with fear, tragedy, starvation and despair. He had lost many of his friends, men who had fought alongside him. Many of these men did not make it home again. The ones who had not become POWs had been killed in subsequent battles, like Crete, El Alamein and Cassino. To a large extent, therefore, the euphoria he felt at being free again, was tinged with deep sadness. He did not know then, but he had a feeling, that his life would never be quite the same again.

The following is an extract from a London newspaper:

"N.Z. V.C. LEADS 'PROCESSION' TO FERNLEAF CLUB"

The sight of Sergeant Jack Hinton, V.C., holding a large Union Jack, which he had acquired in Trafalgar Square, and, followed by hundreds, marching all the way from the square to the Fernleaf Club in Knightsbridge, where packed crowds stood outside cheering for the King, Mr Churchill, and anybody else they could think of, will remain one of the brightest memories of V.E. DAY in London for many New Zealanders. Surrounded by New Zealanders and followed by civilians and men and women in all types of uniform, Sergeant Hinton, who has only recently returned from being a prisoner, thoroughly enjoyed himself, and so did the crowd...."

It was at Margate that Jack met up with Charles Upham again. Upham had been imprisoned in the notorious Colditz Castle – the prison camp the Germans had referred to as "escape-proof". They called it "Sonderlager", or Special Camp. The most troublesome and desperate of all prisoners were sent there for punishment. Upham, the only combatant during the war to win a double V.C. had been repatriated to England shortly after Jack. The war had taken its toll on Upham. He had been severely wounded, nearly losing an arm in the process.

The two men were delighted in meeting each other again. They talked incessantly about their old mates – friends who had been left behind when Crete had received a battering from the Luftwaffe, others who had been overrun by German tanks on the Libyan hill of Belhammed and the disaster at Cassino.

Meanwhile a letter had arrived with a coat of arms on the envelope. It read:

"...The King will hold an Investiture at Buckingham Palace on Friday the 11th May 1945 at which your attendance is requested..."

Jack was allowed to take two guests. He took two girls – one from New Zealand House, the other was the Secretary from the New Zealand Forces Club. Jack went up to London for the Investiture in the company of Charles Upham. The two men were the first to be invested out of a total of perhaps 200. King George VI pinned the real V.C. ribbon on Jack's battledress jacket. It now seemed a long time ago when the German General had pinned the replica on to his army shirt in POW camp.

CENTRAL CHANCERY OF
THE ORDERS OF KNIGHTHOOD,
ST JAMES'S PALACE, S.W.1.

2nd May 1945.

CONFIDENTIAL.

Sir,

The King will hold an Investiture at Buckingham Palace on Friday, the 11th May, 1945, at which your attendance is requested.

It is requested that you should be at the Palace not later than 10.15 o'clock a.m. (Doors open at 9.45 a.m.)

DRESS:—Service Dress; Morning Dress; Civil Defence Uniform or Dark Lounge Suit.

This letter should be produced by you on entering the Palace, as no further card of admission will be issued.

I am desired to inform you that you may be accompanied by two relations or friends to witness the Investiture, but I regret that owing to the limited accommodation available for spectators, it is not possible for this number to be increased. The spectators' tickets may be obtained on application to this Office and I have to ask you, therefore, to complete the enclosed form and return it to me immediately.

I am, Sir,
Your obedient Servant,

[signature]

Secretary.

Sergeant J.D. Hinton,
V.C., New Zealand Military Forces.

159

"Well, Sergeant Hinton" His Majesty said. "Congratulations on receiving this award. Tell me, did the Germans feed you well?"

"We were half-starved most of the time, sir" said the thin ex-POW.

The South Island Infantry Depot was at Broadstairs in Kent and one day in June many members from 20 Battalion were gathered together there. Sergeants Basil Borthwick and Bill Allison, former prisoners of Stalag VIIIA in Gorlitz, East Germany, were in the same Mess.

Jack was wearing his V.C. ribbon alongside his Africa Star, and Bill, all innocence, asked him if he could see the actual medal. Jack gave him a funny look and said: "I've never shown it to anyone before. I'll show it to you, but if you tell anybody, I'll knock your bloody head off!"

Jack was very much like most New Zealand men of that time – reticent about parading his achievements.

The ships were sailing for New Zealand. The flood of released Kiwi prisoners, all 9,000 of them, waited eagerly for their posting to one of them.

Another telegram arrived at the Hinton residence in Colac Bay.

"7930 Sergeant J.D. Hinton (V.C.) in draft Number 425 (stop) You will be advised on disembarkation concerning his future movements."

DEFENCE

One can imagine the excitement that day in the small neat house in Southland.

In the meantime reports on the conduct of Sergeant John Daniel Hinton were pouring into Base Records, Wellington, through various channels.

"The following statement by 6425 WO II James C.E. 2 NZEF regarding the abovenamed soldier is forwarded for attachment to his personal record.

"I have the honour to report on the conduct of Sgt. J.D.

160

HINTON whilst he was a prisoner-of-war in Germany. Sgt. HINTON in Stalag 9C kept the boys in a good state of morale, made himself unpopular with the Germans as a result of constant consideration for the men, especially New Zealanders. Sgt. HINTON also made one escape but unfortunately through a railway accident he was recaptured before being able to leave the country."

On 3 July, 1945 Jack set sail from Liverpool for New Zealand. At long last he was going home. On board were many of his old mates from Dunedin. The ship landed at Wellington on a very wet day – it was 4 August. When he realised there was a battery of cameras to be faced when he left the ship, Jack immediately tried to be as elusive as possible. According to a newspaper article at the time he was

"about his own pursuits 'somewhere aboard' when the ship came alongside, and it was only by persuasion of the ship's public address system that he made his way back to his cabin to be greeted by the very thing he had doubtless been trying to avoid – a couple of pressmen with cameras.

He was with friends, however, cabin mates and so on....they provided some affinity for the retiring Sgt. Hinton, who is from Colac Bay, Southland.

From the citation for this, the first New Zealand V.C. of this war, it is evident that Sgt. Hinton's cross was as well earned as any, and the 'Post' was informed that his conduct was such at the time that a German officer's report contrib uted to the decision to grant the highest award.

After the initial camera flashes in his cabin, the ship's most highly honoured serviceman was about to relax a little – he cannot get used to adulation and publicity, especially after nearly four years in a prison camp – when the Prime Minister arrived. A few more flashes and a few informal words with his mates, and Sgt. Hinton was whisked off, once more to be lost in the turmoil of a big ship – more than 1500 people on board – undergoing disembarkation pains...."

"'...A grand chap' said one of his fellow Kiwis. 'The finest on the ship.'"

Fred Jones, Minister of Defence, accompanied Peter Fraser in welcoming home the returned men. Jack was put up at the Grand Hotel, Wellington, and then caught the overnight ferry to Lyttelton. From Lyttelton he caught a train to Invercargill. He was getting nearer to home by the minute. But he was not to be allowed to arrive quietly. First of all he had to get through a Mayoral reception for all the returned men. Jack remembers seeing a truck decorated in ferns. After the reception his sister and brother-in-law drove him to Riverton. It was good to be back in his beloved South Island again. It was such a contrast to what he had experienced as a POW in war-torn Europe.

On to Colac Bay – could he really be going home, after so long, after all he had been through? Germany, the cold, the hunger, the dying, the men – all a lifetime away. He wondered if his mother would recognise him? He was aged, much thinner, and old, so old – years away from the healthy, fit and happy young man who had farewelled his parents years before – only five years earlier, yet it seemed 20 or more.

The car drew up outside his parents' home in the main street. The street seemed smaller and narrower than he remembered. Maybe he had been away too long. Sudden flashes from his childhood came rushing back to him – he and his boyhood friends running down the street, fishing in the local stream, the pretty young schoolmistress, Miss Frederick, the bees, the back garden.

And so it was that the old man of 35 stood in front of his childhood home looking at the neat garden, the scrubbed front steps. A lump came to his throat. He walked up the path and suddenly he saw the figure of his mother. She seemed smaller and frailer, her hair more grey than he remembered. She was wearing a flowered apron. Was it new? She was hanging the washing on the line, trying to control the sheets as they blew fiercely in the cold winter's wind. He stood for a moment watching her. Suddenly she turned around putting her hand over her eyes, shielding them from the bright winter's sun. Jack tried to say something, but no words came out. He wanted to shout "Mother!" She came forward, her last steps a run. She held her arms out to him, and he fell into them, burying his face in her hair, as tears flowed down her face wetting his battle dress.

Back in the old living room that he had last seen in December, 1939, Jack relaxed for the first time since he was back in New Zealand. He sank in to the comfortable sofa, drinking tea and eating his mother's home-baked cakes. There were, of course, the inevitable questions, his mother's worries about his health, and as always, his desire to put her fears at rest. He was well again now, although he still could not eat a normal diet, and he really hadn't done anything extraordinary – the other chaps had done just as much as he.

There were one or two humorous moments, such as going to the tobacconists for cigarettes in Invercargill where he wasn't recognised. He was refused and told by the owner: "No, you certainly can't have any! Don't you know there's a war on?"

However, at another shop he saw a fellow he knew before the war who generously gave him a whole carton.

There were difficult occasions which he was forced to endure while at home in Colac Bay. The people of Southland threw a huge 'welcome home' function for Jack in the large Colac Bay hall. The welcome was not confined to Colac Bay residents only – many people from Southland, and as far away as Invercargill, gathered to fill the hall to capacity. As a newspaper cutting reported, "It was one of the biggest gatherings ever seen at Colac Bay." A large number of Maori were present and a feature of the proceedings were songs of welcome sung by a party of Maori women.

In addition to Jack, three other returned men, Private P. Kini, Driver R.J. Kelland and Private A. Kelland, were also guests of honour. Each man was presented with a framed certificate, suitably worded and bearing a photograph of the soldier.

The Maori people were proud of the high honour bestowed on Jack, and they too made a presentation to him. Each of the guests of honour briefly replied. Jack had been dreading the fact that he would be called on to make a speech. He kept it short and sweet, saying there was one thing he could not do and that was make speeches. He thanked them all for their wonderful welcome and the people of the surrounding district, for the way they had turned out.

The following speech by Dr. C.H. Gordon of Riverton was recorded in *The Southland Times*.

"On the happy occasion of your homecoming to the country you have served with such distinguished gallantry, it is the wish, not only of your own district, but also of all Southland to convey to you some expression of the pride which we feel in your valour.

You were one of the first of New Zealand's sons to respond to the call to arms in September, 1939, and in the army the qualities of self reliance and enterprise which you had earlier shown on the field of sport, soon won you promotion in the historic campaign in Greece, a lost battle which did more than we know to win the war, you fought with a brave company, tenacious in the face of bitter odds.

It was at the end of that action, when men's courage might well have failed, that you showed the great fighting spirit which won you the highest award that bravery can earn.

On Saturday, October 18, 1941, Southland was filled with pride at the announcement that His Majesty the King had been graciously pleased to approve the award of the Victoria Cross to Sergeant John Daniel Hinton of the 20th Battalion of the N.Z. Military Forces.

...The people of this province, indeed all your countrymen rejoiced in your release from the hands of the enemy and admired your determination to return to action. We are doubly glad now that you have returned to your birthplace and we wish you all the blessings of health, long life and happiness in the country you have served so honourably and well."

Other tributes came pouring in from around the country:

"I have read most of the citations of the V.C. winners in this war, and in almost every case it states that the award has been made for great courage and leadership. A soldier is never rewarded for a foolhardy act, but when a desperate situation develops as was the case at Kalamata, Greece, it is the man who has the courage to take all the risks, and who has the ability to lead others, who is invaluable to any fighting force. There is just such a man...and that is Jack Hinton. His gallant act may have given that little bit of extra time which made all the difference between threats and a disaster and may have saved hundreds of lives."
— Deputy Mayor of Invercargill

Some of his old Kiwi cobbers from before the war weren't at all surprised when they heard of his award.

"Jack was frightened of nobody," said Bill Diedrichs. "I know how tough he was."

After spending about a week with his family, Jack went up to Christchurch for a joyous reunion with Eunie. For nearly six years she had waited patiently for him, worried about him, prayed for him. Eunie had made a deliberate decision to wait until after Jack had met his family before seeing him again. She was at the railway station to meet him. There seemed to be crowds of people, all eagerly awaiting the returned men. She was nervous, not knowing what to expect. She saw him suddenly in amongst the crowd of khaki-clad figures. He was surrounded by people, and then he saw her. She was wearing a smart woollen suit, a little black hat perched on top of her curly dark hair. He waved excitedly. She wanted to run towards him but she hung back shyly. There were too many people, too much noise. He pushed his way through the crowd and all of a sudden he was standing before her – thin, tired-looking, and somehow much older. For just a second there was silence, neither one of them knowing quite what to say. Then suddenly his face broke into his old grin, and the years melted away. They both started to talk at once, then they laughed and the ice was broken. He was home.

Reunited with Eunie he was truly back home again.

–12–
A NEW LIFE

"AH, MAKE THE MOST OF WHAT WE YET MAY SPEND,
BEFORE WE TOO INTO THE DUST DESCEND; DUST INTO
DUST, AND UNDER DUST, TO LIE, SANS WINE, SANS
SONG, SANS SINGER, AND – SANS END!"
– RUBAIYAT OF OMAR KHAYYAM –

All returned Kiwi men came home to a tumultuous welcome, not only from their families but also from a grateful Government. They were given free travel around New Zealand, low interest housing loans, assistance into business or training in professions, and help to go on the land. More than 10,000 ex-servicemen were assisted in becoming farmers.

For a time after returning home, Jack was restless, unable to decide what to do. He found it difficult to settle down after his four long years as a prisoner-of-war, and wondered if he too, should go on the land and farm. While he was making up his mind as to what he should do, he was hospitalised for further treatment of his war wounds. He weighed only 50 kilograms and was still on a light diet.

When Jack was released from hospital, he and his mother went to Invercargill. Both of them envisaged a quiet trip – a time for rest and relaxation. Instead it turned into a nightmare which left both of them exhausted and irritable. Jack was immediately recognised wherever he went; the fuss and publicity was still fresh from the award of his V.C. Mary Hinton knew that people wanted to let her son know that they were proud of him and only wished to welcome him back to Southland. However, she decided she would not accompany him on any further trips. As for Jack, it was to be a taste of things to come.

Wherever he went he was cornered by the press. Would he give an interview on the exploits which won him the Cross? He declined. What about his impressions on prison life? That was a different story. But it was hard going for he was naturally shy and retiring. The papers called him "the reluctant hero". Some things he wanted to keep to himself, perhaps forever. His mates understood what it had been like. They had been there. They had seen the chaos, the devastation, they had suffered the indignities of prison life – the lack of food, clothing, they had witnessed torture, death. It was all there in his mind, and it would be a long time before those scenes would fade.

There was something else which bothered him. When he was pressed by some tiresome reporter on why he thought he had won the most coveted medal of them all, he would reiterate that the medal should have gone to the men who had fought alongside him – men like Alan Jones, Jim Hesson, Doug Patterson, Bob O'Rorke, Pat Rhind.

"They were wonderful men" he would say. "Congratulate them, not me. I had my war cut short. My mates went on to fight more battles. They are the real heroes."

It bothered him in a very real sense that he had been taken prisoner, that he had not gone on to fight for Crete, Minquar Qaim, Ruweisat Ridge.

When he met up with some of them again after the war – those men who had come back – and he heard about the shocking atrocities and what they had suffered, he wondered why he had been singled out. And he thought about his mates who had not come back, many of them in their early twenties in the prime of their lives. One of his old mates from the West Coast who had fought all through the Greek and Crete campaigns, and in Libya and in Italy, told him a story one day. After returning home, he had gone to his local pub for a quiet drink. After one or two drinks, he had tried to convey something of what he had personally gone through to the publican. The publican had called him "a bloody liar" and to get out of his hotel! That was not an isolated incident. Similar happenings had occurred to other returned men. One soldier was so distraught after coming home and seeing the same fat sparrows perched on the power lines, the same countryside untouched by war, and seeing the disbelief on people's faces, that he took a shot-gun and killed himself.

Jack tried to convey something of this to the press, but it was to be a long time before people understood what the returned men had gone through.

Eunie and Jack's mother, Mary, the two women who loved him more than anyone else, and knew him more than anyone else, sensed something of what Jack felt. They knew he was restless, unable to settle. He was distressed and embarrassed at the adulation he received from his countrymen. He conveyed something of what he was feeling to someone he knew would understand. That man was Charles Upham, a man even more reticent and reserved than Jack. Upham knew what Jack was going through. He himself was continually besieged by reporters wherever he went, and at one stage, he locked himself in his house, refusing to come out.

Jack spoke to Charles quietly one day. Both men had a deep sense of justice, and an abhorrence of cruelty and brutality. It was Upham's wish that he be allowed to go back to Germany and hunt down some of the Nazi criminals. He had been imprisoned in the notorious Colditz Castle and his file there was over four inches thick and marked: "Has an incorrigible hatred of the German people."

At Colditz there was one particular SS corporal in the Death's Head Hussars. He was rotten to the core and Upham told him that he was on the "Schwarzliste" (German for Black List.) He told Upham he would do him in before he left. He never got the opportunity because Colditz was liberated soon after. Jack thought the idea a good one – he had a few scores he would like to settle himself, and he felt he should be involved in something of the same. But it was not to be for either man. The British would not allow Upham to return to Europe, and Jack was declared unfit by a medical board. There was nothing for it but to accept the situation.

In October 1945 Jack was invited to a Government function for all winners of the Victoria Cross. The telegram read as follows:

Sgt Hinton V.C. has been invited attend Government function Wellington 11 Oct in uniform Stop Contact him and if not already in possession of uniform in good condition issue him with new battle dress.

Army

Jack, in the company of 10 other surviving Victoria Cross winners of World War I and World War II, attended the State luncheon in Wellington. The luncheon was held in honour of New Zealand winners of the V.C. in the World War II. Parliament specially adjourned to mark the occasion. Walter Nash deputised for Prime Minister Peter Fraser who was unwell. Nash spoke feelingly of the debt due to the servicemen, and the special regard the country had for its greatest heroes. Then after a toast proposed by him, and seconded by the then Leader of the Opposition, Sidney Holland, Charles Upham was called on to reply on behalf of the other V.C. winners present.

Speaking sincerely, Charles began by saying that the only circumstances that had brought him to the function was that he was the representative of 100,000 others whose exploits were as fitting of the reward as his. "Those exploits were only made possible through the sacrifice of others" he said.

He continued on to extol the virtues of the New Zealand soldier. "One thing I want to ask...when these men come back, people who are in a position to do so should show their thanks in a practical way. There will be among them men who are maimed, still suffering from wounds, ill, or mentally ill. They'll need homes, furniture and jobs. Please show them your practical help and your greatest patience."

When Jack returned to Christchurch he and Eunie ran into Bill Wright, a representative for Dominion Breweries. He knew Jack was at a loose end, and suggested that he go to Auckland to see Sir Henry Kelliher, the Managing Director. He and Eunie caught the boat to Wellington and the train to Auckland where they were met by Sir Henry.

Kelliher was impressed with Jack. He sensed certain qualities

170

in the man – trustworthiness, capability, inflexibility of purpose. He also had a sense of humour, enthusiasm. What better man for the job? Would Jack be interested in running one of his hotels? Indeed he would. It would be something he could get his teeth into. Perhaps it would be like the old days before the war. Jack asked only one thing – that Eunie could go with him, and be his housekeeper. Kelliher agreed wholeheartedly.

"You can have any hotel you like!" he told Jack. What was it he had read recently about the man? That's it. "A bloody fine joker, the salt of the earth." They were right. He was sure he had summed Hinton up correctly. He would be exactly right for the hotel business. He knew he had made the right decision. But should he give him the Thistle? The place was a dive, a real run-down joint.

"I've got a place in mind, but it's pretty seedy."

"I don't mind," said Jack. "Give me any one you like."

Kelliher looked at him. Steely blue-grey eyes, a determined set of the jaw, rugged features and as thin as a rake. The man smoked constantly. "Probably gave the Jerries hell," thought Kelliher. Typical Southerner. "I almost pity the poor sods".

Jack and Eunie took over the infamous Thistle Hotel on the corner of Derby and Queen Street early in 1946. It was known as the wildest hotel in Auckland. As one "old dig" put it: "It was a hot bed for criminals, prostitutes and the underworld. People had a lot of respect for Jack, and he seemed the logical choice to run such an establishment. If anyone could create order out of such a place, he certainly could."

When Jack was at the Thistle numerous customers would go in and ask him if Jack Hinton was about. He would ask them if they knew him, and they would say they were great mates of his, so Jack would point to somebody else and say that was him!

Jack had eight barmen, and most of them were jockeys. He recalls two in particular – Jack McRae and Topsy Turvey. They were particularly popular with the customers. Topsy Turvey was a good steeple and hurdles chaser.

The Thistle was so rough in those days that there was a fight in almost every glass of beer. Every night as it got closer to 6 o'clock (when the pub closed) the noise got louder and the drinkers became more aggressive. At one stage it became so bad that Jack had to ban certain customers.

In April, 1946 there was one further award for Jack – a Mention in Despatches for his escape attempts. In addition to his V.C. he now had the MID Emblem, the 1939-45 Star, North Africa Star, Defence Medal, War Medal, and the N.Z. War Service Medal. The MID emblem meant more notoriety, more publicity.

By April every returned man was home – those who were ever to come home. It was a time for celebration, and the men of 20 Battalion and Armoured Regiment decided it was a good time to hold their first reunion.

The reunion was arranged to coincide with the return to New Zealand of Major-General Howard Kippenberger, its original commanding officer. Kippenberger, known to all as "Kip", and beloved and revered by all, had been severely wounded in Italy near the end of the war, losing both feet to a landmine. The reunion was held on the 24th of May in Christchurch and two Air Force planes brought the men from all over New Zealand. The Wentworth Cabaret had been hired for the occasion, and publicity about the reunion had been spread throughout New Zealand.

Newspapers covered the reunion, the first of its kind.

"....The largest reunion of any New Zealand Army Unit which fought in the Second World War was held in Christchurch last night when more than 700 former members of the 20 Battalion from many parts of New Zealand assembled to welcome back their first commanding officer. As he entered the Wentworth Hall to attend the reunion, Major-General Kippenberger walked between long lines of men of his old battalion standing to attention, and as he reached the dais he was greeted with prolonged cheering....For a few hours on Saturday the 20 Infantry Battalion the South Island's first fighting unit of the 1939-45 war, lived again. More than 700 men who fought in its platoons or tank squadrons in the campaigns of Greece,

Crete, North Africa and Italy paraded in Latimer Square and marched through Christchurch streets to attend commemoration services for their fallen comrades...."

Brigadier Jim Burrows in his toast to the 20th spoke of how the 20th had produced men of which it could be justly proud. They included Captain Charles Upham, V.C. and Bar, Sergeant Jack Hinton, V.C. and 2nd Lieutenant Jack Denvir who had performed remarkable feats with the Yugoslav partisans.

Eric Townley of Christchurch who organised the reunion today recalls that first reunion and the financial problems they had:

"The organising committee had very little idea of income or expenditure" he says. "On the night of the reunion I was sitting at a table with a worried look, and a host of accounts which were more than we could meet. A gentleman (not of the 20th, and unknown to me) came up to me and said: 'You look a bit worried'. I said I was, and that I could end up in jail if unable to meet costs. He asked me the value of the major account which was beer, and he took it off me and I never saw it again. He said he would take it from me because of Kip – not the 20th. I never knew the identity of that man."

After three years at the Thistle Hotel Jack and Eunie transferred to the Waikato hotel in Hamilton east. This was later known as the Riverina Hotel. It was December 1949 and the Labour Party had been voted out and the National Party had been elected as the Government. National had passed a law allowing for the first time Maori women to drink in the hotels and to have equal rights with other New Zealanders. The first day Jack took over was a Saturday, and before long numerous Maori women entered the lounge. It wasn't too long before a steward found Jack and told him to look in the lounge. Jack was astonished to find the Maori women seated on the floor eating mussels, crayfish and pauas, and told them they would have to leave. He went around to the

Public Bar where their menfolk were drinking, and he asked the biggest of them who was in charge. He informed Jack in no uncertain terms that he was head of the group, and Jack told him that the women would have to go. The big Maori replied that women had equal rights now but Jack told him that they may have equality with the Government but unless they removed the children and the food off the floor they would have to go. Before long they all left. A week or so later they all returned and he had no further bother.

The 1950s brought a decade of general prosperity, peace and contentment. It was also a time of great political change. The National Party which had been voted in at the end of 1949 and its Prime Minister, Sid Holland, was to become famous for the watersiders' strike of 1951. That same year Holland called an early election and National won again. This election was also notable for the fact that Maoris could vote for the first time on the same day as Europeans.

New Zealand became more independent as a nation, even though it still had close ties with Britain. Farming boomed and prospered and the country became a world leader in social welfare. The elderly, the infirm, the unemployed (of which there were very few) were all looked after by the state.

News of New Zealand's buoyant economy spread to the rest of the world. It attracted many immigrants, including Jack's old mate from his prisoner-of-war days, Dennis Gallagher. Gallagher wrote to Jack telling him he was emigrating to New Zealand. The two old friends had a joyful reunion. They sat up many a night recounting their adventures. Dennis confided in Jack that the England that he returned to in 1945 was not the same as the one he had left. He also had a wanderlust in him brought on by his wartime service that was not easily quelled.

Gallagher fell in love with New Zealand, especially the South Island, and he spent as much time as possible seeing as much of the country as he could. It was on one of these trips, a bus tour of the North Island, that he met a woman who turned out to be a millionairess. The two eventually married. He worked for the

Post & Telegraph in Christchurch and then joined "K-Force" troops in Korea. He and his wife eventually settled in Ireland.

In 1952 Jack took over Kells Hotel in Cobden. He was a popular manager and the hotel was the centre for the sporting clubs of the district. In the bar gathered members of the Cobden Rugby League, Rugby Union, Bowling and Cricket clubs, the Greymouth Defence Rifle club, and the Cobden Marching Team.

Jack provided assistance and trophies for any other organisations needing help. He became an executive member of the Defence and Bowling Clubs and kept a fatherly eye on the others. To his way of thinking, the hotel fulfilled its proper function in the community. It wasn't just a place to drink, it was also a centre from which the recreational activities of the district were run. Many of the clubs held their meetings in the lounge with Jack providing surprise suppers.

In the 1950s the West Coast was still very isolated – its young men worked hard, mostly in the mines and they rarely had the chance to travel. Jack had a wage and savings scheme for the men. Every pay day the men handed in a portion of their wages to him. He banked this ready for their annual two-week football trip. He was a great believer in the men having the opportunity to travel, even if it was only throughout their own country. He was always mindful of the fact that if it had not been for the war he probably would not have had the chance to travel himself. Why wait for another one, he thought, before these lads could see the sights too?

While Jack was living at Cobden and managing Kells he made many good friends, including Lindsay Abbie. Lindsay owned the local grocery shop, and like Jack, had a great sense of humour.

Lindsay Abbie was a talented musician and played the violin for the famous West Coast band "The Kokotahis" for many years. Jack and Lindsay remained firm friends until his death in 1994.

In Cobden George Taylor was the local cop. As was the case with many sleepy towns such as this one, the rules were relaxed from time to time. It usually took George until 11 o'clock at night to check the hotels (there were two at Cobden) and to clean them

175

out of customers. A distance of some 200 metres separated the two pubs. When George had checked the first pub, the proprietor would ring Jack at Kells and tell him that George was on his way. Jack would shout: "Out boys!" and they would immediately scarper out the back door as George came through the front.

Just before Jack acquired Kells Hotel he was given a special present from a friend in Auckland. They were packing up ready to leave for the South Island and a taxi driver called on them to say there was someone in the taxi wanting to see Jack. When he went outside he couldn't see anybody, but when he looked into the taxi he saw a tiny fox terrier, just a few months old sitting on the back seat. It was love at first sight for the two of them. Jack named him Gunner and the little dog refused to leave his side. He was a perfect guard dog, for someone only had to go near Jack for the dog to snarl. If anybody touched the dog he would bite, as Sid Holland found out one day when he bent down to pat Gunner! If Gunner was left alone he was alright, but one day one of Jack's customers kept blowing in Gunner's face. Gunner finally had enough. He snapped at the man's nose and split it!

One night Jack and Eunie stayed in the Midland Hotel in Wellington. He took Gunner up to his room in a zipped-up bag, unknown to the hotel staff. The next morning when the house-maid came in with tea and biscuits, she nearly dropped the tray with astonishment when Gunner appeared from under the blankets! Jack explained to the maid that he was taking Gunner down to the South Island, and she went down to the kitchen and returned with a bone for him.

Dogs were not allowed in hotels and Jack was in constant fear of Gunner being discovered by the authorities. He knew that if caught he would have to give him away. A friend of Jack's who lived in Hamilton offered to take Gunner, and Jack reluctantly parted with him. The separation did not last long though. Jack was miserable without him and he needed very little persuasion from Eunie to get him back again.

Gunner was so attached to Jack and Eunie that he could never be parted from either of them. Unfortunately it meant that they could never go away together for a holiday without Gunner, as one of them would have to stay behind to look after him. Gunner was with Jack until he died at the grand age of 18 years.

The year 1953 was momentous for two events – the Coronation of Queen Elizabeth II and the conquest of Mt Everest by New Zealander Edmund Hillary. Jack was part of the New Zealand contingent who were invited to the Coronation. The New Zealanders flew from Auckland to Sydney and joined the HMS *Sydney* aircraft carrier to England.

Jack found the accommodation on the ship far from good, with the men having to sleep in hammocks, and the food not very good either. They were all pleased to finally arrive in Plymouth where they caught the train to Surrey. They rehearsed for a few weeks for the Coronation procession in Surrey. A day or two before the Coronation they marched along the route in pouring rain. On the day itself Jack led the procession with the Flag Bearer of the New Zealand Contingent.

Jack returned to New Zealand on the *Captain Hobson* along with a few hundred immigrants to "the new country". Jack had a great time telling them all about New Zealand and they seemed eager to learn.

On arrival back in New Zealand his mates clamoured around him wanting to know about the famous people he had met.

"What's the Queen like, Jack? What did she say to you?

"Did you see Monty?"

Jack answered all the questions as best he could, pleased to be finally back home again. "The Queen Mother? She's very down-to-earth, a smashing person".

In 1956 Jack took another journey overseas when the Victoria Cross and George Cross Celebrations were held in London. With the other New Zealand holders of the Cross Jack flew to England in a Royal New Zealand Air Force transport plane. Jack Grant was one Victoria Cross winner from the World War I who was there also. He had won his V.C. in 1918 in France. On the first evening they were all required to attend a function presided over by Lord and Lady Mountbatten. Jack arrived in the company of

Jack Grant and Harry Laurent who had won his V.C. in France in 1918 also. Laurent had regaled the two Jacks with stories of how he was related to the Prime Minister of Canada, St. Laurent. At the hotel where they were all staying, Grant had had rather a lot to drink and by the time they arrived at the function he was rather the worse for wear. As he went through the door, he spied Lord and Lady Mountbatten in full regalia. Grant went up to Lady Mountbatten and slapping her heartily on the back greeted her with a "How are you, Edwina?" He shook hands with Mountbatten and then went over to the bar. He threw some pound notes down on the counter and said: "I'll shout the bar!" With that he fell over a table! There was no bar of course, the drinks were free!

Unknown to Grant, Bernard Freyberg, in charge of the New Zealand contingent, had been watching.

He motioned to Jack who was trying to hide in a corner.

"Hinton!" he called out in his high-pitched voice. "Grant's shickered. Get him out of here!"

With the help of Harry Laurent, Jack managed to get Grant into a car driven by an A.T.S. girl. Jack rode back in the car to the hotel and the A.T.S. girl helped him put the inebriated Grant to bed.

"We won't hear any more from him tonight," said Jack to the girl. "What time do you get off work tonight?"

She told him she would be free in a couple of hours.

"We'll go on a pub crawl," said Jack.

When Jack met up with her again a short time later, they went down to the bar for a drink, and who should be propping it up but Jack Grant! He was perched on a stool, as large as life, with a rum in his hand and looking as if butter wouldn't melt in his mouth!

The years were passing. Jack and Eunie married after her husband Albert died. From 1956 onwards they returned to live privately in Christchurch. They took Nell McGrath, who had been their housemaid at Kells to live with them. She was a real character, who loved to bet on the horses.

For a time Jack ran the bottle store in Greshams Hotel in Cashel Street, Christchurch and then he and Eunie bought the lease of the Templeton Hotel on the Main South Road. While they were there they met up with many great trotting men. One in particular was Derek Jones, who is still a great mate of Jack's today. Jones is an owner-driver breeder, and had two famous horses – "Hands Down", who won the New Zealand Cup and "Blossom Lady". He has lived at Templeton since 1949.

Derek Jones says Jack was a most popular publican. "He was a real man's man, and he ran a good friendly hotel. The only time I saw him really upset was when a fellow who was always a nuisance around town, annoyed one of the ladies. Jack jumped the bar and the man took off!"

One day Jack went to Riccarton to collect Eunie's electric sewing machine which had been repaired. He arrived back at the hotel at lunch time, put the machine behind the bar and began to serve customers. There were many freezing workers in the bar, and one of them asked him what he had put behind the bar. Jack told him it was a typewriter as he was writing a story about conversations he had heard over the years in the bar.

The following day one of the Union Executives came into the hotel and told Jack he had received a complaint that he was writing what he heard in the bar. Jack took the man out to the kitchen and convinced him that it was only a sewing machine.

When Jack left the pub at Templeton the whole town showed up and showered him with presents. Today, they still have fond memories of Jack.

Jack and Eunie stayed in the hotel business, moving up and down the two islands. They made more friends and renewed old friendships. One old friend whom he met up with again was Basil Carey, whom he first met in Kalamata. Carey was holidaying in the South Island, staying on the West Coast and in Dunedin. He and his wife stayed with Jack and Eunie, before eventually settling in Perth.

In 1958 Jack and Eunie bought the lease of the Plough Hotel in Rangiora. At first business was rather slow, and some days Jack would sit outside on the footpath. One day a couple of children came by. He talked to them and bought them a raspberry and lemonade. The following day they brought along some friends and before long, he had some 20 children lined up after school!

Rangiora was a great farming district. Jack met up again with his friend Bill Diedrichs who had a sheep farm at West Belt. He had known Bill and his family from Kokatahi on the West Coast since the 1930s. Jack Diedrichs, Bill's father, used to drive cattle from Harihari to the Red Hutt, stay overnight, and then truck them to Ross.

Bill says Jack never made any money at the Plough – he gave it all away, mostly to charitable organisations. One or two of the Plough's characters in those days were Bill Palmer and Lance Heron. Palmer lived on his own and grew gherkins. He was a great fellow for port wine and Eunie would make soup for him and leave it at the end of the bar. Lance Heron would bring in sides of lamb and buckets of peas from his garden for Eunie and Jack. Rangiora had about 3,000 people then, and after Jack left the district they named a street after him – Hinton Place.

Then there were people like Elsie and Norman Churchill who worked for the Hintons. Norman worked in the bar and Elsie was the chef, and a very good one too.

On the 19 December, 1963 Jack was in the bar with some friends. He noticed that the time was just on 6 o'clock and he went through to the kitchen. There slumped on the floor was Eunie. She had suffered a heart attack. Frantically he rushed back to the bar. The Churchills, together with George Loffhagen, and Jed Morris were there. They tried desperately to resuscitate her, but nothing could be done. Eunie, so dear to Jack, his laughing, vivacious, gentle Eunie, had died at the age of 66.

Jack was broken-hearted by the death of Eunie, and in early 1964 when the lease at the Plough Hotel ran out, he decided to return to his home in Clyde Road, Riccarton. A friend of his, Colin Berkett, had just bought the Rolleston Hotel, and he asked Jack if he would give him a hand until he was broken in. Colin and his wife were good friends, and of course Jack would always help a mate. Jack worked at the Rolleston Hotel until the end of May, when it was time for him to get ready to return to London for the Victoria Cross and George Cross Reunion there. One Saturday night he went into the city for a meal, and as he walked back to his car in Latimer Square, he was set on by three thugs. They beat him up and robbed him of some money, his passport and his watch. The *Christchurch Star* recounted the incident:

"Victoria Cross winner, Mr Jack Hinton, was beaten up in Latimer Square in the heart of Christchurch and robbed of four pounds...still bore heavy bruises today from the attack.

Mr Hinton said that he had a meal in a city cafe on Saturday night, and as he crossed the square afterwards three youths intercepted him.

"I had no chance" he said. "All I could use were my boots." He still had heavy bruises on his back and face and two black eyes. He was also kicked in the pit of the stomach. Mr Hinton said he thought the youths had seen him pull his money from his pocket in the cafe, and had followed him to the square.

...Mr Hinton only recently relinquished the licence of the Plough Hotel in Rangiora.

He won his V.C. in Greece in 1941 while serving with the 2nd NZEF."

Jack had to get a new passport quickly and new dentures were fitted when he arrived in London.

Towards the end of 1964, Jack Hinton rang Sir Henry Kelliher's office. He was looking for another hotel to manage.

"Come up to Auckland and see what you want!" said Kelliher. Jack chose the Ponsonby Club Hotel, taking over from Harold Ellerington. But he was there for only two weeks, because unexpectedly the position of manager at the D.B. Hotel in Onehunga became vacant. It was perfect for Jack and he soon settled in. He had a good staff, especially Bill McEwan, who was his Assistant Manager.

Jack had his eyes opened at the Onehunga pub. He saw women

fighting each other there – something he had never seen before.

One other time Jack was attacked by a man wielding a tomahawk. He was saved in the nick of time by a young Maori boy who rushed in.

Besides Bill McEwan and his wife, Mata, who was Jack's cook, a good friend was Doug Brown, who took over as Assistant Manager when the McEwan's went down to the South Island. In 1970 when Jack did a spot of relieving in other hotels, Doug managed the Onehunga and was there for many years.

When Jack first arrived back in Auckland in 1964, he couldn't wait to go to the Trots again – he had always had a keen interest, and in 1966 he became a Member. The following year he was elected as a Steward of the Club, and in 1968 was elected to the Committee. He served on the Board until 1980 when he retired to Ashburton. It was in that year he was made a Life Member of the Club. This was a special honour and it was bestowed on him for his exceptional services to the Club. Recently, he received a Certificate of Service stating that he had been a Member for 30 years.

Jack enjoyed his years with the Auckland Trotting Club. There were five Presidents while he was there. There was Percy Bridgens, then Reg Lewis. Reg and Jack raced a couple of horses together. Then there was Merv Corner, who had been a half-back for the All Blacks many years ago, Dr John Sullivan and Ron Robertson. Ron and Jack were elected to the Committee at the same time, along with Albert Brownson and Tom Antonovich. Jim Patterson succeeded Alf Forrest as Secretary and he is now the Chief Executive Officer.

Jack spent every available moment at the races and had, indeed still has, a great relationship with every old trainer in the country. They all know him and respect him, and in the trotting establishment he gets red carpet treatment everywhere he goes. As he was in the hotel trade, Jack was responsible for setting up the Club's bar operation, and he oversaw this side of the Club's activities for many years. He was the first person to put tills into the trotting clubs. Previously Colemans the caterers held the lease of the bars, but Jack took it away from them so the clubs could get all the profits.

The Trotting Club staff used to be amused at the sight of Jack during the 6 o'clock closing days going from bar to bar, and standing in the centre of the room shouting "Time gentlemen, please!"

Jack was renowned for his hospitality and looked after many visiting trainers when they brought horses to Auckland to race. It was a feature of their trip to Auckland to stay with Jack and some very late nights were had at the Onehunga Hotel.

Back in 1943, a young woman called Molly Schumacher had just left school and was working in a sharebroker's office in Christchurch. Her employer was also the Secretary for the Prisoner-of-War enquiry office. Molly was kept busy attending to all the POW business. Next-of-kin would go into the office and pay for items like chocolates, for example, which went into the Red Cross parcels, and she would take the orders over to the Red Cross rooms in Cathedral Square. While she was working at the POW enquiry office, she came across the names of Charles Upham and Jack Hinton. There were about 1400 POWs from Canterbury and Westland, and about 200 men held prisoner by the Japanese who could not receive parcels. Once a month she would send out newsletters to the next-of-kin.

Years later, in 1964, Molly was working at the Clarendon Hotel in Auckland for Maurice Murphy. When the Clarendon closed down in 1966, Molly was left without a job. It was while she was looking for another that she ran into an old friend of hers, Bill McEwan, who worked for the Onehunga Hotel. Would there be a possibility of a job there for her? Bill promised to do what he could; he would have to ask the boss.

It took only one short telephone call to George Armstrong at the Hotel Workers Union from Jack to secure a place for Molly at the Onehunga Hotel. Molly started work on Monday, 22 August, 1966 in the club bar and on the 22 February, 1968 after they had known each other for exactly 18 months, Molly and Jack were married.

Jack and Molly continued to manage hotels, mainly in the North Island. In the early 1970s they relieved at places like the

Esplanade in Devonport, the D.B. Tavern in Wellesley Street, the Newmarket, the Riverina in Hamilton East, the Franklin, De Bretts in Taupo, and the D.B. at Turangi.

In 1980 they sold their flats in Epsom, Auckland, and retired to Ashburton. They decided to settle in Ashburton as over the years they had stayed with friends Harry and Julie Harrison, firstly at their farm in Methven, then at Ashburton, and they had been on many fishing trips with Harry and his friends. Jack loved going to Lake Coleridge in early November for the opening of the land-locked salmon and rainbow trout season. About eight of them stayed in Harry's hut where he had his own electric power plant. It was a good life. Jack enjoyed the fishing, then at night they would have dinner, a few drinks, play cards and tell yarns, then turn in early, as they would be up before daylight.

Over the years there were many such fishing trips with people like Harry and Dudley Harrison, Doug Dalton, Bill Talbot, and Bert Stevens. They fished for salmon in the Rakaia and Rangitata Rivers and down near Twizel. Harry Harrison was a great fisherman, and as he was nearly always the first to catch a fish. He was nicknamed "Harry the Hook".

On 17 September, 1989 Jack turned 80. Over 120 friends from all over New Zealand attended the birthday celebrations in the Ashburton R.S.A. Lounge. Molly, in the company of two of his 20th Battalion mates, Jack Bishop and Bernie Dynes, organised the function. The friends fell into three groups; friends from Ashburton and surrounding districts, friends from the New Zealand Trotting fraternity, and lastly, friends from ex-service organisations.

Peter Wolfenden, the well-known trotting reinsman who drove four New Zealand Trotting Cup winners, including the great Cardigan Bay in 1963, and J.K. Hughes came from Rotorua, Derek Jones from Templeton, and Eugene McDermott from Halswell. Eugene's son John, Jack's godson, also attended. John McDermott was celebrating his 40th birthday on the same day as his godfather was celebrating his 80th.

Many 20 Battalion people attended, including Charles and Molly Upham, Brigadier Jim Burrows, 'Gentleman Jim' to all,

Doug Eggleton who had enlisted with Jack in Greymouth, with his wife Phyl, the artist Austen Deans, and his wife Liz, past and present Presidents of the 20th Association, and a host of others. A grand time was had by all.

It was during these 80th birthday celebrations that Jack received a letter from the granddaughter of Fritz Hahn, his old POW guard at Muhlhausen. The letter was addressed as follows:

"Jack Hinton,
Cala Bay, Southland,
New Seeland."

It finally reached the Hintons in Ashburton.

This was to be the start of a long correspondence between the Hintons and the Hahns, culminating in a trip to Germany in 1990 for Jack and Molly. In that first letter to Jack from Stefka, Hahn's granddaughter, she asked Jack if he remembered her grandfather. Indeed he did, and when they met up in Hahn's home town of Eisenberg, East Germany, it was a joyous reunion for them both. It was 45 years since they had seen each other. Jack had been given to understand that when the war ended Fritz had been shot by the Americans.

In one letter to the Hintons Stefka wrote:

"...We are very happy about your visit. It was for us a very nice time, and you teach me more English. But the two weeks was too fast. We hope you like this time, and we hope Jack can forget the dark bad times at 1944-45 Muhlhausen."

In 1990 Jack and Molly left Ashburton and moved closer in to Christchurch where they live in the suburb of Bexley, close to Molly's sister and brother-in-law, Murita and Allan. They have a delightful garden and it is a constant source of pleasure for them both. Friends continually drop by; he has remained in close contact with all his old mates, the ones who are left from his early days, and his post-war life. His friendships made in wartime have been lifelong ones. He never passes an old 20th mate in the street without stopping for a yarn.

Jack has always remained down-to-earth. Kipling's famous quotation: "If one can walk with Kings nor lose the common touch" – this so applies to Jack. As Derek Jones puts it:

"Jack just loves people. He has no enemies. He is such a good-natured man. I have never heard a word said against him, and that's not because he won the V.C. He doesn't differentiate between adults and children – he loaned all his medals to my nephew once."

Jack has always had a strong sense of justice. The first on the scene if a mate is in a spot of trouble. Some years after the war ended Jack heard that one of the 20th Battalion men was down on his luck. He had lost his job and had three young children to feed. Without hesitation, Jack put fifty pounds into an envelope and dropped it into the man's letterbox.

Jack has always been a positive person. He has strong opinions on many issues, but is healthily critical. He is "switched on" regarding past and current affairs. He presents a picture of a man who is deeply thoughtful, quiet, intelligent, loyal, and obstinate with a real dislike for humbug. What you see is what you get – "a straight shooter" according to one of his mates. He has a strong sense of humour, and a surprising softness towards children and animals. The children of his mates naturally gravitate towards him. A surprising number of people are drawn to him, disarmed by his personality.

For more than 25 years Jack has met his old friends at the R.S.A. Bowling Tournament in Tauranga which is named in his honour. More than 300 players from around the North Island contest the bowls tournament in February each year.

Recently a plaque was erected at the Christchurch R.S.A. which bears his name – the John Daniel Hinton restaurant. Above the doorway of the entrance to the dining room is a photograph of him as a young soldier in uniform.

Overseas trips have been largely curtailed now, although he still manages a trip or two. In 1995, he managed two trips to London for the 50th Anniversary celebrations to commemorate the end of World War II. He was also invited to the Royal Tournament Victory at Earls Court. On occasions when Jack has been in England for the reunion of the V.C. and George Cross winners, he always looks up old friends, some of whom have now passed away. One of these close friends was Hugh Watt, former Deputy Prime Minister and Minister of Electricity in the Labour Government and for some years before his death, High Commissioner in London.

One day in the 1970s when Jack was running the Newmarket pub – and Norman Kirk was Prime Minister and Hugh Watt was Deputy Prime Minister – an Australian barman went up to Jack and said:

"There's some joker out there claiming to be the Deputy Prime Minister. He says he wants to talk to you."

"What's his name?" asked Jack.

"Watt!" said the barman.

"Bring him in!" said Jack.

"Hugh was one of the nicest fellows I ever met" says Jack. "He was a great Liberal."

The two men were friends until the day Watt died.

Today, when pressed by journalists on the circumstances of his winning the Victoria Cross, he is deliberately vague.

"It's too long ago now. I have forgotten." Forgotten! This has always been his stock answer. Sometimes I would catch him unawares, sitting quietly in his armchair, a look in his eye which told me he was far away. I wondered if he was thinking about the battlefields of Kalamata, in far-off Greece where he had fought so long ago with his mates. Or perhaps he was thinking of the long journey he had made over 50 years ago, a journey which had started in Burnham Camp in 1939 to the heat and dust of Egypt, and to a country where he could smell the sweet scent of herbs in the air. Could he still see the blood-stained battlefield, hear the cries of his wounded mates, feel again the starvation and the cold of the "con" camp and the other camps in Germany? Was he remembering the four long years in captivity, and the uncertainty of whether he would see his loved ones again? Or perhaps it was the years after the war – the struggle to begin a new life again, of "fitting in" to civvie life, of people he had loved and befriended – all gone now – Kip, Jim Burrows, Charlie Upham – the other men of the 20th, George Brown and Jack Bain, and the others who had fought alongside him – Alan Jones, who had lost both legs to amputation, Jim Hesson, Pat Rhind and most of all, his mother, and his laughing dark-haired Eunie. Perhaps he was listening to the echo of their voices down the years -

"Fancy a brew-up, old bean, what?"

"Look at that lovely little piece over there! I wouldn't mind taking her out!"

"Shut up, Jack! She'll only go out with officers!"

"And I saw her first!"

"To hell with this! Who will come with me?"

"For you the war is over!"

Jack has never lost the ability to laugh at himself or see the funny side in any situation. Perhaps that has been the key to his survival. His health is as good a can be expected for a man of his age, and he loves to relax in the evening with a cigarette and a glass of Scotch. Molly looks after him, fusses over him, and still calls him darling after nearly 30 years of marriage.

"Come on, Jack," she says. "Tell us about the time when..."

And out it all comes, after a passage of 60 or 70 years.

I will leave the last words to William Shakespeare:

> ## "HE WAS A MAN, TAKE HIM FOR ALL IN ALL, I SHALL NOT LOOK UPON HIS LIKE AGAIN!"
> – WILLIAM SHAKESPEARE –
> HAMLET ACT 1 SCENE 2

INDEX

189

Palmer, Bill 180
Parrington, Brigadier 77, 80, 81, 89, 90
Paterson, R.D.B., Major 54
Patterson, Doug 82-84, 87, 88, 91, 168
Patterson, Jim 182
Pemberton, Major 16, 81
Plough Hotel 179-181
Ponsonby Club Hotel 181
Pringle, David 53
Prouse, Robert 141-142

Riverina Hotel 173, 184
Riverton 18, 20
Rhind, Patrick, Captain 82, 83, 88, 91, 168, 188
Robertson, Ron 182
Rolleston Hotel 180
Rommel, Erwin, General 73
Ruweisat Ridge 168

Salonika 187, 106-111, 115, 116
Savage, Mickey 46, 49-51, 53, 57, 64
Semple, Bob 44, 46, 51, 53
Simmonds, Captain 82
Simpson, J. 120, 121, 127
Sobieski 58, 59
Spicer, Jack 71
Stalag Luft 115, 146
Stalag Villa 160
Stevens, Bert 184
Stott, Donald, Major 107
Sullivan, John, Dr 182

Talbot, Bill 184
Taylor, George 175, 176
Templeton Hotel 179
Thistle Hotel 171, 173
Thomas, Bill 22
Thomson, G.H., Major 85, 87, 90, 93, 103, 104
Thompson, Albie 78, 87, 89-91

Townley, Eric 173
Turvey, Topsy 171

Upham, Charles V.C. & Bar 13, 14, 55, 101, 113, 114, 158, 169, 170, 173, 183, 184, 188

Wallace, Mervyn 148
Wallace, Spike 142
Watt, Hugh, Sir 187
Wavell, General 67
Webb, Paddy 53
Whitehead, Stan 44
Wilson, C., Captain 114
Wing, 153
Wolfenden, Peter 184
Wright, Bill 170

Zannas, Madame 96